UNITED STATES INTELLIGENCE COMMUNITY

COLLABORATUS VIRTUS FIDES

INTELLIGENCE AND CRIME
TERMINOLOGY

A glossary of terms and acronyms
2015

DAVID CARIENS

HighTide
Publications, Inc.

Copyright © 2015 by David Cariens.

High Tide Publications, Inc.
1000 Bland Point Road
Deltaville, Virginia 23043
www.HighTidePublications.com

Ordering Information: Quantity sales. Special discounts are available on quantity purchases by corporations, associations, and others. For details, contact the "Special Sales Department" at the address above.

Intelligence and Crime Terminology A Glossary of Terms and Acronyms/ David Cariens /1st ed.
Subject Heading: Dictionaries
BISAC REF0080000

Printed in the United States of America

ISBN 9780692384237

Note to Readers

All statements of fact, opinion, or analysis expressed in this book are those of the author and do not reflect the official positions or views of the Central Intelligence Agency (CIA) or any other U.S. Government agency. Nothing in the contents should be construed as asserting or implying U.S. Government authentication or information or CIA endorsement of the author's views. This book has been reviewed by the CIA to prevent the disclosure of classified information.

Introduction

During my nearly 50 years of working in intelligence and crime analysis, I have compiled a list of words, acronyms, and abbreviations associated with the profession. About a year ago, it dawned on me that pulling together the most frequent terms, with their definitions, might make a useful resource for all analysts.

These definitions come from a large number of United States Intelligence Community members. I do, in some instances, give alternative definitions and indicate from what area or field they come from, such as crime analysis or the military. When I found close definitions of the same word from a number of organizations, I defaulted to the CIA or National Counterterrorism Center definitions. In a few cases I have reworked the definitions to make them fit a wider number of intelligence agencies. Unfortunately when I began making the list I had no idea that someday I would try to publish it, so I cannot identify where I got all the definitions for the acronyms.

I plan on updating and/or correcting the list annually. If anyone reading this has additional words or acronyms, and their definitions, to suggest please contact me. The same is true if you find any errors.

Given the size of the U.S. Intelligence Community, I am sure I have left out something. I also know that intelligence terminology is not stagnant. So please help me make the list more complete and useful.

I hope you find this a useful publication beneficial and helpful for your work.

David Cariens
Kilmarnock, Virginia
January, 2015
Contact: dcariens@davecariens.com

Preface

An acronym is an abbreviation formed from the initials of the words in a phrase or word. In most instances, the acronym is comprised of individual letters (as in *NATO* or *laser*) or parts of words or names (as in *Benelux*).

There is no universal standardization of styling for acronyms, or their style. In this document we have capitalized the acronyms in most instances. However, the style guide for your organization may suggest an alternative methodology which you should follow.

Some of the acronyms in this book are a registered trademark. We have made every effort to indicate such entries by using the trademark symbol ™. However, in no way should this be considered to be a complete list of trademarked entries.

There are two sections to the acronym and definition listings. The first is an alphabetical listing of the acronym and its definition. The second section is an alphabetical listing of definitions and their corresponding acronym.

Acronyms and definitions highlighted in grey indicate an expanded definition is listed in the glossary.

Acronyms

Section 1 – Alphabetical listing by Acronym with corresponding definition

Acronym	Definition
A	
AAG	Associate Attorney General
ABA	American Bankers Association
ABA	American Bar Association
ACA	American Correctional Association
ACJA	American Criminal Justice Association
ACLU	American Civil Liberties Union
ACS	Automated Case System (FBI)
ACTIC	Arizona Counter Terrorism Information Center
ADA	Assistant District Attorney (or Americans with Disabilities Act)
AFIS	Automated Fingerprint Identification System
AFMLS	Asset Forfeiture and Money Laundering Section, Department of Justice
AG	Attorney General

Acronym	Definition
APB	Advisory Policy Board or All-Points Bulletin
APEC	Asia-Pacific Economic Cooperation
APPA	American Probation and Parole Association
ARJIS	Automated Regional Justice Information System
ASAC	Assistant Special Agent in Charge (FBI)
ASCA	Association of State Criminal Investigative Agencies
ATAC	Anti-Terrorism Advisory Council
ATF	Bureau of Alcohol, Tobacco, Firearms and Explosives
ATIX	Automated Trusted Information Exchange
ATTF™	Anti-Terrorism Task Force (FBI)
AUSA	Assistant U.S. Attorney
B	
BATFE	Bureau of Alcohol, Tobacco Firearms and Explosives

Acronym	Definition
BJA	Bureau of Justice Assistance
BJS	Bureau of Justice Statistics
BOP	Federal Bureau of Prisons
BSA	Bank Secrecy Act
BSA	Bank Secrecy Act (FinCEN-related)
BSAAG	Bank Secrecy Act Advisory Group

C

Acronym	Definition
C3	Command Control Communication
CAD	Computer-Aided Dispatch
CALEA	Commission on Accreditation for Law Enforcement Agencies
CapWIN	Capital Wireless Integrated Network
CAT	Communities Against Terrorism
CATIC	California Anti-Terrorism Information Center

Acronym	Definition
CBR	Chemical, Biological, Radiological
CBRNE	Chemical, Biological, Radiological, Nuclear, and Explosive
CCH	Computerized Criminal Histories
CDC	Centers for Disease Control
CenTF	Center for Task Force Training
CEO	Chief Executive Officer
CERT	Computer Emergency Response Team
CFR	Code of Federal Regulations
CFTC	Commodity Futures Trading Commission
CHFI	Committee on Hemispheric Financial Issues
CHRI	Criminal History Record Information
CI	Confidential Informant or Criminal Intelligence or Counter Intelligence (the latter being the Intelligence Community use of CI)

Acronym	Definition
CIA	Central Intelligence Agency
CICC	Criminal Intelligence Coordinating Council
CICE	Criminal Intelligence for the Chief Executive
CIKR	Critical Infrastructure and Key Resources
CIO	Chief Information Officer
CIP	Critical Infrastructure Protection
CISA	Criminal Information Sharing Alliance
CISAnet	Criminal Information Sharing Alliance Network
CJIS	Criminal Justice Information Services
CJNet	Criminal Justice Network
CMIR	Currency and Monetary Instrument Report.
CODIS	Combined DNA Index System
COI	Community of Interest

Acronym	Definition
COMINT	Communications Intelligence
CompStat	Computerized Statistics
ConOps	Concept Operations
COOP	Community of Operations Plan
CTISS	Common Terrorism Information Sharing Standards
CTR	Currency Transactions Reports
CTRC	Currency Transactions Reports by Casinos
CUI	Controlled Unclassified Information
D	
DA	District Attorney
DAG	Deputy Attorney General
DAISH	DAISH is an acronym [Arabic: Al-Dawlah Al-Islamiyah fe Al-Iraq wa Al-Sham]
DEA	Drug Enforcement Agency

Acronym	Definition
DELJIS	Delaware Justice Information System
DHHS	U.S. Department of Health and Human Services
DHS	Department of Homeland Security
DHS	Department of Homeland Security
DIA	Defense Intelligence Agency
DNI	Director of National Intelligence
DNI-U	Director of National Intelligence-Unclassified
DOC	Department of Corrections (U.S. Department of Commerce)
DoD	U.S. Department of Defense
DOJ	U.S. Department of Justice
DOL	U.S. Department of Labor
DOR	Department of Revenue
DOS	U.S. Department of State

Acronym	Definition
DOT	U.S. Department of Transportation
E	
EMS	emergency medical services
EOC	emergency operations center
EOP	Executive Office of the President
EOUSA	Executive Office for United States Attorneys
EPA	Environmental Protection Agency
EPIC	El Paso Intelligence Center
F	
FAA	Federal Aviation Administration
FATF	Financial Action Task Force on Money Laundering
FBAR	Foreign Bank Account Report
FBI	Federal Bureau of Investigation

Acronym	Definition
FCG	Fusion Center Guidelines
FDIC	Federal Deposit Insurance Corporation
FEMA	Federal Emergency Management Agency
FI	Field Interview/Field Interview Card
FIAT	Foundations of Intelligence Analysis Training
FIG	Field Intelligence Group
FinCEN	Financial Crimes Enforcement Network (Treasury Department)
FIP	Fair Information Practices
FIR	Field Review Report
FLETC	Federal Law Enforcement Training Center
FOIA	Freedom of Information Act
FOUO	"For Official Use Only" information handling caveat
FSF	Financial Stability Forum

Acronym	Definition
G	
G.R.E.A.T.	Gang Resistance Education and Training
GAC	Global Advisory Committee
GATT	General Agreements on Tariffs and Trades
GCC	Gulf Cooperation Council
GFIPM	Global Federated Identity Privilege Management
GHSAC	Governors Homeland Security Advisory Council
GIS	Geographic Information Systems
GIWG	Global Intelligence Working Group
GJXDM	Global Justice XML Data Model
Global	Global Justice Information Sharing Initiative
GPS	Global Positioning System
H	

Acronym	Definition
HIDTA	High Intensity Drug Trafficking Area
HIDTA DIG	HIDTA's Digital Information Gateway
HIFCA	High Intensity Financial Crimes Areas, also called the High Risk High Laundering and Related Financial Crime Area.
HIR	Homeland Information Report
HQ	headquarters
HS	homeland security
HSAC	Homeland Security Advisory Council
HSAS	Homeland Security Advisory System
HSDN	Homeland Secure Data Network
HSGP	Homeland Security Grant Program
HSIN	Homeland Security Information Network
HSIN-CI	Homeland Security Information Network-Critical
HSPD	Homeland Security Presidential Directive

Acronym	Definition
HUMINT	human intelligence
I	
IACP	International Association of Chiefs of Police
IAFIS	Integrated Automated Fingerprint Identification System
IAIP	International Analysis and Infrastructure Protection
IALEIA	International Association of Law Enforcement Intelligence Analysts
IC	U.S. Intelligence Community
ICBA	Independent Community Bankers of America
ICE	Bureau of Immigration and Customs Enforcement, Department of Homeland Security (sometimes referred to as U.S. Immigration and Customs Enforcement)
ICS	Incident Command System
IED	Improvised Explosive Device
IEEPA	International Emergency Economic Act

Acronym	Definition
IEEPA	International Emergency Economic Powers Act
IICT	Interagency Intelligence Committee on Terrorism
III	Interstate Identification Index
IIR™	Institute for Intergovernmental Research or Intelligence Information Report (FBI)
IJIS	Integrated Justice Information Systems
ILEA	International Law Enforcement Academy
ILO	International Liaison or Industry Liaison Officer or Intelligence Resource Specialist
ILP	Intelligence-led Policing
IMAP	Intelligence Mutual Aid Pact
IMF	International Monetary Fund
IMM	International Monetary Market
INCSR	International Narcotics Control Strategy Report
INCSR	International Narcotics Control Strategy Report

Acronym	Definition
INL	Bureau of International Narcotics and Law Enforcement Affairs, Department of State
INTERPOL	International Criminal Police Organization
IRS	Internal Revenue Service, Department of the Treasury or Intelligence Research Specialist
IRS-CI	Internal Revenue Service-Criminal Investigations-Department of Treasury
IRTPA	Intelligence Reform and Terrorism Prevention Act of 2004
ISAC	Information Sharing and Analysis Center
ISDN	Integrated Services Digital Network
ISE	Information Sharing Environment
ISE-SAR	Suspicious Activity Report (with terrorism nexus)
ISIL	Islamic State of Iraq and the Levant also translated as ISIS (Islamic State of Iraq and Syria)
IT	information technology
ITACG	Interagency Treat Assessment Coordination Group

Acronym	Definition
ITACG	Interagency Treat Assessment Coordination Group
J	
JAG	Judge Advocate General or Justice Assistance Grant Program
JIEM	Justice Information Exchange Model
JOM	Japanese Offshore Market
JRIES	Justice Regional Information Exchange System
JTFE	Joint Terrorism Task Force
JTTF	Joint Terrorism Taskforce (FBI)
K	
KWIC	Key Word In Context
L	
LAWINT	Law Enforcement Intelligence
LEA	Law Enforcement Agency

Acronym	Definition
LECC	Law Enforcement Coordinating Committee
LEIS	law enforcement information sharing strategy
LEIU	The Association of Law Enforcement Intelligence Units
LEO	Law Enforcement Online
LES	Law Enforcement Sensitive-Information (handling caveat)
LETPP	Law Enforcement Terrorism Prevention Program
LIFFE	London International Financial Futures Exchange
LLIS	Lessons Learned Information Sharing

M

Acronym	Definition
MAGLOCLEN™	Middle Atlantic-Great Lakes Organized Crime Law Enforcement Network
MALWARE	Malicious Software
MCC	Major Cities Chiefs Association
MCSA	Major County Sheriff's Association

Acronym	Definition
MI-5	Military Intelligence, Section 5 Britain's internal security service (BSS)
MI-6	Military Intelligence, Section 6
MIPT	Memorial Institute for the Prevention of Terrorism
MLCA	Money Laundering Control Act 1986
MLCC	Money Laundering Coordination Center, Department of Homeland Security
MLSA	Money Laundering Suppression Act of 1994
MOCIC	Mid-States Organized Crime Information Center (Trade Mark)
MOU	Memorandum of Understanding

N

Acronym	Definition
NACIC	National Counterintelligence Information Center
NARA	U.S. National Archives and Records Administration
NCB	National Central Bureau (U.S. contact for INTERPOL)
NCIC	National Crime Information Center

Acronym	Definition
NCIRC	National Criminal Resource Center
NCIS	Naval Criminal Investigative Service or National Criminal Intelligence Service (United Kingdom)
NCISP	National Criminal Intelligence Sharing Plan
NCJA	National Criminal Justice Association
NCSL	National Conference of State Legislatures
NCTC	National Counterterrorism Center
NCUA	National Credit Union Administration
N-DEx	Law Enforcement National Data Exchange (FBI)
NDIC	National Drug Intelligence Center
NDPIX	National Drug Pointer Index
NESPIN™	New England State Police Information Network
NFB	National Intelligence Board
NFCCG	National Fusion Center Coordinating Group

Acronym	Definition
NFIB	National Foreign Intelligence Program
NGA	National Geospatial-Intelligence Agency or National Governors Association
NGB	National Guard Bureau
NGIC	National Gang Intelligence Center
NIC	National Intelligence Committee
NICC	National Infrastructure Coordinating Center
NIE	National Intelligence Estimate
NIEM	National Information Exchange Model
NIJ	National Institute of Justice
NIMA	National Imagery and Mapping Agency, an Intelligence Community agency
NIMS	National Incident Management System
NIO	National Intelligence Officer
NIPC	National Infrastructure Coordination Center

Acronym	Definition
NIPP	National Infrastructure Protection Plan
NJTTF	National Joint Terrorism Task Force
NLETC	National Law Enforcement Training Center
NLets	The International Justice and Public Safety Network
NOC	National Operations Center
NPD	National Preparedness Directorate
NRIG	Northeast Regional Intelligence Group
NSA	National Sheriffs' Association or National Security Agency
NSC	National Security Council
NSD	National Security Directive
NSOPR	National Sex Offender Public Registry
NSOPW	National Sex Offender Public Website
NSOR	National Sex Offender Registry

Acronym	Definition
NW3C	National White Collar Crime Center
NYSE	New York Stock Exchange
O	
OAS	Organization of American States
OCC	Office of Comptroller of the Currency, Department of Treasury
OCDETF	Organized Crime Drug Enforcement Task Force
ODNI	Office of the Director of National Intelligence
OECD	Organization for Economic Cooperation and Development
OEM	Office of Emergency Management
OFAC	Office of Foreign Assets Control
OFC	Offshore Financial Center
OGBS	Offshore Group of Banking Supervisors
OJP	Office of Justice Programs, Department of Justice

Acronym	Definition
OMB	Office of Management and Budget
ONDCP	Office of National Drug Control Policy
OPCOM	Open Communications
ORCON	Originator Controlled
OTS	Office of Thrift Supervision, Department of Treasury
P	
P3I	Public-Private Partnerships for Intelligence
PART	Program Assessment Rating Tool
PDB	President's Daily Briefing
PERF	Police Executive Research Forum
PFIAB	President's Foreign Intelligence Advisory Board
PKI	Public Key Infrastructure
PM-ISE	Office of the Program Manager, Information Sharing Environment

Acronym	Definition
PPP	Public-Private Partnership
R	
RAC	Resident Agent in Charge
RCPI	Regional Community Policing Institute (of COPS)
RDD	Radiological Dispersal Device
R-DEx	Regional Data Exchange (FBI)
RFI	Request for Information
RFP	Request for Proposal
RFS	Request for Service
RICO	Racketeer Influenced and Corrupt Organizations Act) (Criminal Intelligence)
RISS ATIX™	RISS Automated Trusted Information Exchange
RISS DES	RISS Data Exchange Specification
RISSafe™	RISS Officer Safety Event Deconfliction System

Acronym	Definition
RISSNET™	Regional Information Sharing Systems Secure Intranet
RISS™	Regional Information Sharing Systems
RMIN™	Rocky Mountain Information Network (Trade Mark)
RMS	Records Management System
ROCIC™	Regional Organized Crime Information Center
RTTAC	Regional Terrorism Threat Assessment Center
RTTF	Regional Terrorism Task Force (FBI)
	S
S.W.I.F.T.	Society for Worldwide Interbank Financial Transactions
SAA	State Administrative Agency
SAC	Special Agent in Charge (FBI)
SAR	Suspicious Activity Report
SAR	Suspicious Activity Report - Financial Intelligence

Acronym	Definition
SAR	Suspicious Activity Report (Criminal Intelligence)
SAR-C (Financial Intelligence)	Suspicious Activity Report for Casinos and Card Clubs
SAR-MSB (Financial Intelligence)	Suspicious Activity Report for Money Services Businesses
SAR-SF (Financial Intelligence)	Suspicious Activity Report for Securities and Futures Industries
SBU	Sensitive But Unclassified
SCCs	Sector Coordinating Councils
SCI	Sensitive Compartmented Information
SCIF	Sensitive Compartmented Information Facility
SEARCH	The National Consortium for Justice Information and Statistics
SEIB	Senior Executive Intelligence Brief (CIA intelligence summary for senior U.S. government officials).
SEOC	State Emergency Operations Center
SHSI	Sensitive Homeland Security Information

Acronym	Definition
SIG	Special Interest Group
SIGINT	Signals Intelligence
SIPNET	Secret Internet Protocol router Network
SLATT™	State and Local Anti-Terrorism Training
SLT	State, Local, and Tribal
SOP	Standard Operating Procedure
SSA	Senior Special Agent or Supervisory Special Agent
SSCI	Senate Select Committee on Intelligence
T	
TA	Technical Assistant
TC Project	Trusted Credential Project
TCL	Target Capabilities List (DHS)
TEW	Terrorism Early Warning Group

Acronym	Definition
TLO	Terrorism Liaison Office
TPEP	Terrorism Prevention Exercise Program (DHS)
TS	Top Secret
TS/SCI	Top Secret/Special Compartmented Intelligence
TSA	Transportation Security Administration

U

Acronym	Definition
UASI	Urban Areas Security Initiative
USA	United States Attorney or (with periods) United States of America
USAO	United States Attorney's Office
USBP	United States Border Patrol
USC	U.S. Currency, U.S. Citizen, or United States Code
US-CERT	United States Computer Emergency Readiness Team (DHS)
USCG	United States Coast Guard

Acronym	Definition
USMS	United States Marshals Service
USPS	United States Postal Service
USSEC	United States Securities and Exchange Commission
USSS	United States Secret Service, Department of Homeland Security
V	
VGTOF	Violent Gang and Terrorist Organization File
VICAP	Violent Criminal Apprehension Program
W	
WB	World Bank
WIRe	World Intelligence Review
WMD	Weapons of Mass Destruction
WSIN™	Western States Information Network

Acronyms

Section 2 – *Alphabetical listing by definition with corresponding acronym*

Acronym	Definition
A	
APB	Advisory Policy Board or All-Points Bulletin
ABA	American Bankers Association
ABA	American Bar Association
ACLU	American Civil Liberties Union
ACA	American Correctional Association
ACJA	American Criminal Justice Association
APPA	American Probation and Parole Association
ATAC	Anti-Terrorism Advisory Council
ATTF™	Anti-Terrorism Task Force (FBI)
ACTIC	Arizona Counter Terrorism Information Center
APEC	Asia-Pacific Economic Cooperation
AFMLS	Asset Forfeiture and Money Laundering Section, Department of Justice
ADA	Assistant District Attorney (or Americans with Disabilities Act)

Acronym	Definition
ASAC	Assistant Special Agent in Charge (FBI)
AUSA	Assistant U.S. Attorney
AAG	Associate Attorney General
ASCA	Association of State Criminal Investigative Agencies
AG	Attorney General
ACS	Automated Case System (FBI)
AFIS	Automated Fingerprint Identification System
ARJIS	Automated Regional Justice Information System
ATIX	Automated Trusted Information Exchange
ATF	Bureau of Alcohol, Tobacco, Firearms and Explosives

B

BSA	Bank Secrecy Act
BSA	Bank Secrecy Act (FinCEN-related)
BSAAG	Bank Secrecy Act Advisory Group

Acronym	Definition
BATFE	Bureau of Alcohol, Tobacco Firearms and Explosives
BJA	Bureau of Justice Assistance
BJS	Bureau of Justice Statistics
BOP	Federal Bureau of Prisons

C

Acronym	Definition
CATIC	California Anti-Terrorism Information Center
CapWIN	Capital Wireless Integrated Network
CenTF	Center for Task Force Training
CDC	Centers for Disease Control
CIA	Central Intelligence Agency
CBR	Chemical, Biological, Radiological
CBRNE	Chemical, Biological, Radiological, Nuclear, and Explosive
CEO	Chief Executive Officer
CIO	Chief Information Officer

Acronym	Definition
CFR	Code of Federal Regulations
CODIS	Combined DNA Index System
C3	Command Control Communication
CALEA	Commission on Accreditation for Law Enforcement Agencies
CHFI	Committee on Hemispheric Financial Issues
CFTC	Commodity Futures Trading Commission
CTISS	Common Terrorism Information Sharing Standards
COMINT	Communications Intelligence
CAT	Communities Against Terrorism
COI	Community of Interest
COOP	Community of Operations Plan
CERT	Computer Emergency Response Team
CAD	Computer-Aided Dispatch
CCH	Computerized Criminal Histories

Acronym	Definition
CompStat	Computerized Statistics
ConOps	Concept Operations
CI	Confidential Informant or Criminal Intelligence or Counter Intelligence (the latter being the Intelligence Community use of CI)
CUI	Controlled Unclassified Information
CHRI	Criminal History Record Information
CISA	Criminal Information Sharing Alliance
CISAnet	Criminal Information Sharing Alliance Network
CICC	Criminal Intelligence Coordinating Council
CICE	Criminal Intelligence for the Chief Executive
CJIS	Criminal Justice Information Services
CJNet	Criminal Justice Network
CIKR	Critical Infrastructure and Key Resources
CIP	Critical Infrastructure Protection

Acronym	Definition
CMIR	Currency and Monetary Instrument Report.
CTR	Currency Transactions Reports
CTRC	Currency Transactions Reports by Casinos
D	
DAISH	DAISH is an acronym [Arabic: Al-Dawlah Al-Islamiyah fe Al-Iraq wa Al-Sham]
DIA	Defense Intelligence Agency
DELJIS	Delaware Justice Information System
DOC	Department of Corrections (U.S. Department of Commerce)
DHS	Department of Homeland Security
DOR	Department of Revenue
DAG	Deputy Attorney General
DNI	Director of National Intelligence
DNI-U	Director of National Intelligence-Unclassified

Acronym	Definition
DA	District Attorney
DEA	Drug Enforcement Agency
DoD	U.S. Department of Defense
DHHS	U.S. Department of Health and Human Services
DOJ	U.S. Department of Justice
DOL	U.S. Department of Labor
DOS	U.S. Department of State
DOT	U.S. Department of Transportation

E

Acronym	Definition
EPIC	El Paso Intelligence Center
EMS	emergency medical services
EOC	emergency operations center
EPA	Environmental Protection Agency
EOUSA	Executive Office for United States Attorneys

Acronym	Definition
EOP	Executive Office of the President
F	
FOUO	"For Official Use Only" information handling caveat
FIP	Fair Information Practices
FAA	Federal Aviation Administration
FBI	Federal Bureau of Investigation
FDIC	Federal Deposit Insurance Corporation
FEMA	Federal Emergency Management Agency
FLETC	Federal Law Enforcement Training Center
FIG	Field Intelligence Group
FI	Field Interview/Field Interview Card
FIR	Field Review Report
FATF	Financial Action Task Force on Money Laundering
FinCEN	Financial Crimes Enforcement Network (Treasury Department)

Acronym	Definition
FSF	Financial Stability Forum
FBAR	Foreign Bank Account Report
FIAT	Foundations of Intelligence Analysis Training
FOIA	Freedom of Information Act
FCG	Fusion Center Guidelines

G

Acronym	Definition
G.R.E.A.T.	Gang Resistance Education and Training
GATT	General Agreements on Tariffs and Trades
GIS	Geographic Information Systems
GAC	Global Advisory Committee
GFIPM	Global Federated Identity Privilege Management
GIWG	Global Intelligence Working Group
Global	Global Justice Information Sharing Initiative
GJXDM	Global Justice XML Data Model

Acronym	Definition
GPS	Global Positioning System
GHSAC	Governors Homeland Security Advisory Council
GCC	Gulf Cooperation Council

H

Acronym	Definition
HQ	headquarters
HIDTA DIG	HIDTA's Digital Information Gateway
HIDTA	High Intensity Drug Trafficking Area
HIFCA	High Intensity Financial Crimes Areas, also called the High Risk High Laundering and Related Financial Crime Area.
HIR	Homeland Information Report
HSDN	Homeland Secure Data Network
HS	homeland security
HSAC	Homeland Security Advisory Council
HSAS	Homeland Security Advisory System
HSGP	Homeland Security Grant Program

Acronym	Definition
HSIN	Homeland Security Information Network
HSIN-CI	Homeland Security Information Network-Critical
HSPD	Homeland Security Presidential Directive
HUMINT	human intelligence

I

Acronym	Definition
ICE	Bureau of Immigration and Customs Enforcement, Department of Homeland Security (sometimes referred to as U.S. Immigration and Customs Enforcement)
INL	Bureau of International Narcotics and Law Enforcement Affairs, Department of State
IED	Improvised Explosive Device
ICS	Incident Command System
ICBA	Independent Community Bankers of America
ISAC	Information Sharing and Analysis Center
ISE	Information Sharing Environment
IT	information technology

Acronym	Definition
IIR™	Institute for Intergovernmental Research or Intelligence Information Report (FBI)
IAFIS	Integrated Automated Fingerprint Identification System
IJIS	Integrated Justice Information Systems
ISDN	Integrated Services Digital Network
IMAP	Intelligence Mutual Aid Pact
IRTPA	Intelligence Reform and Terrorism Prevention Act of 2004
ILP	Intelligence-led Policing
IICT	Interagency Intelligence Committee on Terrorism
ITACG	Interagency Treat Assessment Coordination Group
ITACG	Interagency Treat Assessment Coordination Group
IRS	Internal Revenue Service, Department of the Treasury or Intelligence Research Specialist
IRS-CI	Internal Revenue Service-Criminal Investigations-Department of Treasury
IAIP	International Analysis and Infrastructure Protection

Acronym	Definition
IACP	International Association of Chiefs of Police
IALEIA	International Association of Law Enforcement Intelligence Analysts
INTERPOL	International Criminal Police Organization
IEEPA	International Emergency Economic Act
IEEPA	International Emergency Economic Powers Act
ILEA	International Law Enforcement Academy
ILO	International Liaison or Industry Liaison Officer or Intelligence Resource Specialist
IMF	International Monetary Fund
IMM	International Monetary Market
INCSR	International Narcotics Control Strategy Report
INCSR	International Narcotics Control Strategy Report
III	Interstate Identification Index
ISIL	Islamic State of Iraq and the Levant also translated as ISIS (Islamic State of Iraq and Syria)

Acronym	Definition
ISE-SAR	Suspicious Activity Report (with terrorism nexus)
IC	U.S. Intelligence Community
J	
JOM	Japanese Offshore Market
JTFE	Joint Terrorism Task Force
JTTF	Joint Terrorism Taskforce (FBI)
JAG	Judge Advocate General or Justice Assistance Grant Program
JIEM	Justice Information Exchange Model
JRIES	Justice Regional Information Exchange System
K	
KWIC	Key Word In Context
L	
LEA	Law Enforcement Agency
LECC	Law Enforcement Coordinating Committee

Acronym	Definition
LEIS	law enforcement information sharing strategy
LAWINT	Law Enforcement Intelligence
LEO	Law Enforcement Online
LES	Law Enforcement Sensitive-Information (handling caveat)
LETPP	Law Enforcement Terrorism Prevention Program
LLIS	Lessons Learned Information Sharing
LIFFE	London International Financial Futures Exchange
LEIU	The Association of Law Enforcement Intelligence Units

M

Acronym	Definition
MCC	Major Cities Chiefs Association
MCSA	Major County Sheriff's Association
MALWARE	Malicious Software
MOU	Memorandum of Understanding
MIPT	Memorial Institute for the Prevention of Terrorism

Acronym	Definition
MAGLOCLEN™	Middle Atlantic-Great Lakes Organized Crime Law Enforcement Network
MOCIC	Mid-States Organized Crime Information Center (Trade Mark)
MI-5	Military Intelligence, Section 5 Britain's internal security service (BSS)
MI-6	Military Intelligence, Section 6
MLCA	Money Laundering Control Act 1986
MLCC	Money Laundering Coordination Center, Department of Homeland Security
MLSA	Money Laundering Suppression Act of 1994
N	
N-DEx	Law Enforcement National Data Exchange (FBI)
NCB	National Central Bureau (U.S. contact for INTERPOL)
NCSL	National Conference of State Legislatures
NACIC	National Counterintelligence Information Center
NCTC	National Counterterrorism Center
NCUA	National Credit Union Administration

Acronym	Definition
NCIC	National Crime Information Center
NCISP	National Criminal Intelligence Sharing Plan
NCJA	National Criminal Justice Association
NCIRC	National Criminal Resource Center
NDIC	National Drug Intelligence Center
NDPIX	National Drug Pointer Index
NFIB	National Foreign Intelligence Program
NFCCG	National Fusion Center Coordinating Group
NGIC	National Gang Intelligence Center
NGA	National Geospatial-Intelligence Agency or National Governors Association
NGB	National Guard Bureau
NIMA	National Imagery and Mapping Agency, an Intelligence Community agency
NIMS	National Incident Management System
NIEM	National Information Exchange Model

Acronym	Definition
NICC	National Infrastructure Coordinating Center
NIPC	National Infrastructure Coordination Center
NIPP	National Infrastructure Protection Plan
NIJ	National Institute of Justice
NFB	National Intelligence Board
NIC	National Intelligence Committee
NIE	National Intelligence Estimate
NIO	National Intelligence Officer
NJTTF	National Joint Terrorism Task Force
NLETC	National Law Enforcement Training Center
NOC	National Operations Center
NPD	National Preparedness Directorate
NSC	National Security Council
NSD	National Security Directive

Acronym	Definition
NSOPR	National Sex Offender Public Registry
NSOPW	National Sex Offender Public Website
NSOR	National Sex Offender Registry
NSA	National Sheriffs' Association or National Security Agency
NW3C	National White Collar Crime Center
NCIS	Naval Criminal Investigative Service or National Criminal Intelligence Service (United Kingdom)
NESPIN™	New England State Police Information Network
NYSE	New York Stock Exchange
NRIG	Northeast Regional Intelligence Group
NLets	The International Justice and Public Safety Network
NARA	U.S. National Archives and Records Administration
O	
OCC	Office of Comptroller of the Currency, Department of Treasury
OEM	Office of Emergency Management

Acronym	Definition
OFAC	Office of Foreign Assets Control
OJP	Office of Justice Programs, Department of Justice
OMB	Office of Management and Budget
ONDCP	Office of National Drug Control Policy
ODNI	Office of the Director of National Intelligence
OTS	Office of Thrift Supervision, Department of Treasury
OFC	Offshore Financial Center
OGBS	Offshore Group of Banking Supervisors
OPCOM	Open Communications
OECD	Organization for Economic Cooperation and Development
OAS	Organization of American States
OCDETF	Organized Crime Drug Enforcement Task Force
ORCON	Originator Controlled
P	

Acronym	Definition
PM-ISE	Office of the Program Manager, Information Sharing Environment
PERF	Police Executive Research Forum
PDB	President's Daily Briefing
PFIAB	President's Foreign Intelligence Advisory Board
PART	Program Assessment Rating Tool
PKI	Public Key Infrastructure
PPP	Public-Private Partnership
P3I	Public-Private Partnerships for Intelligence

R

Acronym	Definition
RICO	Racketeer Influenced and Corrupt Organizations Act) (Criminal Intelligence)
RDD	Radiological Dispersal Device
RMS	Records Management System
RCPI	Regional Community Policing Institute (of COPS)
R-DEx	Regional Data Exchange (FBI)

Acronym	Definition
RISS™	Regional Information Sharing Systems
RISSNET™	Regional Information Sharing Systems Secure Intranet
ROCIC™	Regional Organized Crime Information Center
RTTF	Regional Terrorism Task Force (FBI)
RTTAC	Regional Terrorism Threat Assessment Center
RFI	Request for Information
RFP	Request for Proposal
RFS	Request for Service
RAC	Resident Agent in Charge
RISS ATIX™	RISS Automated Trusted Information Exchange
RISS DES	RISS Data Exchange Specification
RISSafe™	RISS Officer Safety Event Deconfliction System
RMIN™	Rocky Mountain Information Network (Trade Mark)

S

Acronym	Definition
SIPNET	Secret Internet Protocol router Network
SCCs	Sector Coordinating Councils
SSCI	Senate Select Committee on Intelligence
SEIB	Senior Executive Intelligence Brief (CIA intelligence summary for senior U.S. government officials).
SSA	Senior Special Agent or Supervisory Special Agent
SBU	Sensitive But Unclassified
SCI	Sensitive Compartmented Information
SCIF	Sensitive Compartmented Information Facility
SHSI	Sensitive Homeland Security Information
SIGINT	Signals Intelligence
S.W.I.F.T.	Society for Worldwide Interbank Financial Transactions
SAC	Special Agent in Charge (FBI)
SIG	Special Interest Group
SOP	Standard Operating Procedure

Acronym	Definition
SAA	State Administrative Agency
SLATT™	State and Local Anti-Terrorism Training
SEOC	State Emergency Operations Center
SLT	State, Local, and Tribal
SAR	Suspicious Activity Report
SAR	Suspicious Activity Report - Financial Intelligence
SAR	Suspicious Activity Report (Criminal Intelligence)
SAR-C (Financial Intelligence)	Suspicious Activity Report for Casinos and Card Clubs
SAR-MSB (Financial Intelligence)	Suspicious Activity Report for Money Services Businesses
SAR-SF (Financial Intelligence)	Suspicious Activity Report for Securities and Futures Industries
SEARCH	The National Consortium for Justice Information and Statistics
T	
TCL	Target Capabilities List (DHS)

Acronym	Definition
TA	Technical Assistant
TEW	Terrorism Early Warning Group
TLO	Terrorism Liaison Office
TPEP	Terrorism Prevention Exercise Program (DHS)
TS	Top Secret
TS/SCI	Top Secret/Special Compartmented Intelligence
TSA	Transportation Security Administration
TC Project	Trusted Credential Project
U	
USC	U.S. Currency, U.S. Citizen, or United States Code
USA	United States Attorney or (with periods) United States of America
USAO	United States Attorney's Office
USBP	United States Border Patrol
USCG	United States Coast Guard

Acronym	Definition
US-CERT	United States Computer Emergency Readiness Team (DHS)
USMS	United States Marshals Service
USPS	United States Postal Service
USSS	United States Secret Service, Department of Homeland Security
USSEC	United States Securities and Exchange Commission
UASI	Urban Areas Security Initiative

V

Acronym	Definition
VICAP	Violent Criminal Apprehension Program
VGTOF	Violent Gang and Terrorist Organization File

W

Acronym	Definition
WMD	Weapons of Mass Destruction
WSIN™	Western States Information Network
WB	World Bank
WIRe	World Intelligence Review

Glossary

A

ATIX

(Criminal Intelligence)

Automated Trusted Information Exchange (Trade Mark) operated by the Regional Information Sharing Systems, ATIX is a secure means of disseminating national security or terrorist threat information to law enforcement and other first responders through the ATIX electronic bulletin board, secure Web site, and secure e-mail.

a priori

relating to or derived by reasoning from self-evident proposition.

Acceptable risk

the level of residual risk that has been determined to be a reasonable level of potential loss/disruption to achieve a level of risk at an acceptable cost.

Access (to sensitive information) (Criminal Intelligence)

sensitive information and/or intelligence may be released by a law enforcement agency when at least one of the following four prescribed circumstances applies to the person(s) receiving the information:

1. **Right to Know** is based on having legal authority, one's official position, legal mandates, or official agreements, allowing the individual to receive intelligence reports.

2. **Need to Know** as a result of jurisdictional, organizational, or operational necessities, intelligence or information is disseminated to further an investigation.

3. **Investigatory Value** intelligence or information is disseminated in the law enforcement community for surveillance, apprehension, or furtherance of an investigation.

4. **Public Value** intelligence or information can be released to the public when there is a need to know and a right to know the information because of the value that may be derived from public dissemination, to (1) aid in locating targets/suspects and (2) for public safety purposes (i.e., hardening targets, taking precautions).

Accountability

the principle that responsibilities for ownership and/or oversight of resources are explicitly assigned and that assignees are answerable to proper authorities for stewardship of resources under their control.

Actionable

intelligence and information with sufficient specificity and detail that explicit responses to prevent a crime or terrorist attack can be implemented. Intelligence that is directly useful to customers for immediate exploitation, often without having to go through the full intelligence production process.

ad infinitum
to infinity; endlessly; without end.

ad hoc

(adv.) For the particular end or case at hand without consideration of wider application.

(adj) Concerned with a particular end or purpose. (An ad hoc investigating committee.)

Administrative analysis (Criminal Intelligence)

is the analysis of economic, geographic, demographic, census, or behavioral data to identify trends and conditions useful to aid the administrators in making policy and/or resource allocation decisions.

Adversary

Any individual, group, organization or government that conducts activities or has the intention and capability to conduct activities detrimental to critical assets.

Agent

Adversaries could include intelligence services of host nations, or third party nations, political or terrorist groups, criminals, rogue employees and private interests.

Agent

1. A person who engages in clandestine intelligence activity under the direction of an intelligence organization but who is not an office employee, or co-opted worker of the organization.
2. An individual who acts under direction of an intelligence agency or security service to obtain, or assist in obtaining information for intelligence or counter intelligence purposes.
3. One who is authorized or instructed to obtain or to assist in obtaining information for intelligence or counterintelligence purposes.

al-Qa'ida-affiliated

use when referring to separate groups, organizations, or individuals who have ties to al-Qa'ida while remaining independent organizations.

al-Qa'ida-associated

use when referring to independent groups, organizations, or individuals who have loose ties to al-Qa'ida.

al-Qa'ida-directed

use when referring to groups, attacks, or events.

al-Qa'ida-inspired

use when referring to self-directed, self-initiated, or self-supported extremists who want to imitate or honor al-Qa'ida. Term is often used to describe homegrown or indigenous extremists.

All-crimes approach
(Criminal Intelligence)

an approach that incorporates terrorism and other high-risk threats into the existing crime-fighting framework, to ensure that possible precursor crimes are screened and analyzed for linkage to larger-scale terrorist or other crimes. This approach recognizes that there is a nexus between types of criminal activity (for example, illegal drug operations, gangs, money laundering, fraud, identity theft, and terrorism). Using an all-crimes approach does not imply that a fusion center must address every single crime that occurs within its area of responsibility. Rather, the routine risk assessment that a fusion center develops or supports developments of should assist in prioritizing which crimes and/or hazards a state or region should address. The assessment should also aid in development of a collection plan and help identify what other sources of information may be useful for examining possible connections with other crimes.

All-hazards approach
(Criminal Intelligence)

refers to preparedness for terrorist attacks, major disasters, and other emergencies within the United

States. (Source HSPD-8, December 13, 2003.) Within the context of the Fusion Process, some fusion centers have defined their mission to include an all-hazards approach. While the application of this approach varies, in general, it means that the fusion center has identified and prioritized types of major disasters and emergencies, beyond terrorism and crime, that could occur within their jurisdiction and gathers, analyzes and disseminates information which would assist the relevant responsible agencies (law enforcement, fire, public health, emergency management, critical infrastructure, etc.) with the prevention, protection, response, or recovery efforts of those incidents. A fusion center can use all-hazards approach but not address in its operations every possible hazard. Part of the annual risk assessment a fusion center develops, or supports development of, should identify which hazards a state or region should prioritize within its homeland security planning process. In addition, it will provide the fusion center with the prioritization needed to develop relevant Priority Information Requirements.

All-Hazards Intelligence

the collection and analysis of information concerned with noncriminal domestic threats to critical infrastructure, community health, and public safety for the purpose of preventing the threat or mitigating the effects of the threat. (Same as Homeland Security Intelligence)

Allocation
(Criminal Intelligence)

is the collection and analysis of information that shows relationships among varied individuals suspected of being involved in criminal activity that may provide insight into the criminal operation and which investigative strategies might work best.

Analysis

that activity whereby meaning, actual or suggested, is derived through organizing and systematically examining diverse information and applying inductive or deductive logic for the purposes of investigation or assessment.

Anarchist terrorists

are opposed to all forms of government; they are often allied with terrorist groups.

Archiving (Records)
(Criminal Intelligence)

the maintenance of records in remote storage after a case has been closed or disposed of, as a matter of contingency, should the records be needed for later reference.

Anti-abortion terrorists

commit acts of terrorism against abortion providers and supporters of the pro-choice movement. Typically motivated by religion in their opposition to abortion, these terrorists frequently target abortion clinics, facilities, and doctors.

Anti-globalization terrorists

oppose the increasing integration of the world into a single free market. They believe that the impact of global capitalism on both the average individual and national culture is negative. Anti-globalization terrorists often target U.S. and corporate interests.

Anti-Terrorism

preventive in nature. It entails using "passive and defensive measures such as education, foreign liaison training, surveillance, and counter surveillance, designed to deter terrorist activities." It is an integrated and comprehensive approach to countering terrorism. The concept has two phases: proactive and reactive. The proactive phase encompasses the planning, resourcing, preventive measures, preparation, awareness education, and training that takes place before a terrorist incident. The reactive phrase includes the crisis management actions taken to resolve a terrorist incident.

Aryan racists groups

are non-Jewish Caucasians, especially of Nordic or Teutonic descent. White supremacist organizations are generally made up of people who are deemed to be sufficiently "Aryan."

Asset

any person, environment, facility, physical system, material, cyber system, information, business reputation, or activity that has a positive value to an owner or to society as a whole. In intelligence, an asset most often refers to a human source.

Association Analysis (Criminal Intelligence)

the entry of critical investigative and/or assessment variables into a two-axis matrix to examine the relationship and patterns that emerge as the variables are correlated in the matrix.

Attractive asset

an asset that has value to an adversary as a desirable target. The nature and magnitude of the value of an asset (what makes it or him or her attractive) to an adversary may differ from the value to the owner.

Critical asset

the criticality of an asset varies depending on the perspective of the analyst. The following definitions are suggested:

Broad societal context – an asset so vital that its incapacity or destruction would have debilitating impact on the local, regional, or national economy or the well-being of society.

General organizational context - an asset whose absence or unavailability would significantly degrade the ability of an organization to carry out its mission.

Functional context for asset owners - an asset whose absence or unavailability would represent an unacceptable business consequence, for which the sum of the consequences of its loss represents an unacceptable financial or political impact on the owner.

Asymmetrical warfare

is warfare in which the two sides are grossly unequal. The less powerful side does not fight the more powerful side under the conventional rules of war because it cannot win by using these tactics. The weaker side uses unconventional methods of fighting such as guerrilla tactics and terrorism

Authentication
(Criminal Intelligence)

the process of validating the credentials of a person, computer process, or device. Authentication requires that the person, process, or device making the request provide a credential proving it is what or who it says it is. Common forms of credentials are digital certificates, digital signatures, smart cards, biometrics data, and a combination of user names and passwords.

Authorization
(Criminal Intelligence)

the process of granting a person, computer process, or device with access to certain information, services, or functionality. Authorization is derived from the identity of the person, computer process, or device requesting access that is verified through authentication.

Audit trail
Criminal Intelligence

a generic term for recording (logging) a sequence of activities. In computer and network contexts, and audit train tracks the sequence of activities on system, such as user long-ins and log-outs. More expansive audit train mechanisms would record each user's activity in detail what commands were issued to the system, what records and files were accessed or modified. Audit trains are a fundamental part of computer security, used to trace (albeit usually retrospectively) unauthorized users and uses. They can also be used to assist with information recovery in the event of a system failure.

B

Ba'ath

literally means "renaissance" in Arabic. The term Ba'ath is generally used in connection with a political ideology that combines secularism, Arab nationalism, and socialism. In Iraq, the Ba'ath party ruled for decades with Saddam Hussein at the helm.

Baseline capability (Criminal Intelligence)

is a capability that provides the means to accomplish a mission or function, resulting from the performance of one or more critical tasks, under specified conditions, to target levels of performance. A capability may be delivered with any combination of properly planned, organized, equipped, trained and exercised personnel that achieves the desired outcome. (Source: *National Preparedness Guidelines,* page 40.) Within the context of this document, a baseline capability for a fusion center is a capability necessary for the fusion center to perform its core functions of gathering, processing, analyzing, and disseminating terrorism, homeland security, and law enforcement information.

Bias/Hate Crime
(Criminal Intelligence)

any criminal act directed toward any person or group as a result of that person's race, ethnicity, religious affiliation, or sexual preference.

Biological or Chemical Agent

saran, mustard, and anthrax are examples of biological or chemical agents. These three examples are not referred to *material* or *weapons.*

Biological or Chemical Weapon(s)

consists of a *biological or chemical agent* mated to a delivery or dissemination system, such as a rocket, bomb, or sprayer.

Biometrics
(Criminal Intelligence)

biometrics methods can be divided into two categories: physiological and behavioral. Implementations of the former include face, eye (retina or iris), finger (fingertips, thumb, finger length, or pattern), palm (print or topography), and hand geometry. The latter includes voiceprints and handwritten signatures.

bona fide

made in good faith, without fraud or deceit. In intelligence, the term is most often used to describe the credibility and truthfulness of a human asset, and is usually referred to as an *assets bona fides.*.

Burqa

is a form of women's clothing that covers the whole body from head to toe, including the eyes, which are hidden behind a mesh veil. Some Muslims believe that women must wear a burqa to comply with Islamic law. The burqa was mandatory for women during the Taliban's rule in Afghanistan.

C

C3

an intelligence application concept initially used by military intelligence that stands for command, control, and communication as the hallmark for effective intelligence operations.

Cadre

a cell of trained personnel around which a larger organization can be built, or a member of such a group, the term cadre is often used to refer to an armed member of a militant or terrorist organization.

carte blanche

full discretionary power

caveat emptor

a principle in commerce: without a warranty the buyer takes the risk of quality upon himself or herself

Capabilities-based preparedness (Criminal Intelligence)

"Preparing, under uncertainty, to provide capabilities suitable for a wide range of challenges while working within an economic framework that necessitates prioritization and choice." (Source: *National Preparedness Guidelines*, page 30.)

Central Intelligence Agency (CIA)

An Intelligence Community agency established to collect, produce, and disseminate foreign intelligence and counterintelligence; to conduct counterintelligence activities abroad; to collect, produce, and disseminate intelligence on foreign aspects of narcotics production and trafficking; to conduct special activities approved by the President; and to conduct research, development, and procurement of technical systems and devices.

Civil liberties (Criminal Intelligence)

fundamental individual rights, such as freedom of speech, press, or religion; due process of law; and other limitations on the power of the government to restrain or dictate the actions of individuals. They are the freedoms that are guaranteed in the Bill of Rights, the first ten Amendments to the Constitution of the United States. Civil liberties offer protection to individuals from improper government and arbitrary governmental interference. Generally, the term "civil rights" involves positive (or affirmative) government action, while the term "civil liberties" involves restrictions on government.

Civil rights
(Criminal Intelligence)

the term "civil rights" is used to imply that the state has a role in ensuring that all citizens have equal protection under the law and equal opportunity to exercise the privileges of citizenship regardless of race, religion, gender, or other characteristics unrelated to the worth of the individual. Civil rights are, therefore, obligations imposed on government to promote equality. More specifically, they are the rights to personal liberty guaranteed to all United States citizens by the Thirteenth and Fourteenth Amendments and by acts of Congress.

Civilian/Non-Combatant

is one who does not bear arms, openly or covertly, in official or unofficial combat during a declared conflict. A civilian does not directly participate in fighting, nor does he or she provide financial, military, or other support to combatants without coercion by force or fear. Indirect political involvement, such as voting in a democracy that wages war, does not deprive one of civilian status. Terrorist groups often target civilians due to the relative ease of the operations, and to maximize the amount of fear caused by the attack.

Civil war

a war within a country rather than between countries; it may be between two or more ethnic groups, political parties, regions or socioeconomic interests. Civil wars are generally fought between factions competing for power over the same political unit. They are also fought to separate one element of a political unit from the main body. Civil wars can take many forms. Some are fought between rival groups of elites. Others are fought between different geographical sections of countries. Others pit socio-economic groups against one another. The principle element is that combatants on both sides consider themselves, or are generally considered to be, of the same political entity.

Clandestine activity

an activity that is usually extensive and goal-oriented, planned, and executed to conceal the existence of the operation. Only participants and the agency sponsoring the activity are intended to know about the operation. "Storefront" operations, "stings," and certain concentrated undercover investigations can be classified as clandestine collection.

Clandestine Operation

a preplanned secret intelligence collection activity or covert, political, economic, propaganda, or paramilitary action conducted so as to assure the secrecy of the operation; encompasses both clandestine collection and covert action.

Classification

the determination that official information requires, in the interest of national security, a specific degree of protection against unauthorized disclosure, coupled with a designation signifying that such determination has been made; the designation is normally termed a security classification and includes Confidential, Secret, and Top Secret.

Classification information/intelligence

a uniform system for classifying national security information, including information relating to defense against transnational terrorism, to ensure that certain information is maintained in confidence in order to protect citizens, U.S. institutions, U.S. homeland security, and U.S. interactions with foreign nations and entities:

Top Secret is applied to information, the unauthorized disclosure of which reasonably could be expected to cause exceptionally grave damage to the national security that the original classification authority is able to identify or describe (Executive Order 12958, March 25, 2003).

Secret is applied to information, the unauthorized disclosure of which reasonably could be expected to cause serious damage to the national security that the original classification authority is able to identify or describe (Executive Order 12958, March 25, 2003).

Confidential is applied to information, the unauthorized disclosure of which reasonably could be expected to cause damage to the national security that the original classification authority is able to identify or describe (Executive Order 12958, March 25, 2003).

Cocalero

a Spanish term referring to growers of coca leaf in South America. Although many coca-growers are peasants, terrorist groups such as the Revolutionary Armed Forces of Colombia (FARC) have also traded in coca and processed cocaine to fund their operations.

Collation (of information) (Criminal Intelligence)

a review of collected and evaluated information to determine its substantive applicability to a case or problem at issue and placement of useful information into a form or system that permits easy and rapid access retrieval.

Collection (of information) (Criminal Intelligence)

the identification, location, and recording/storing of information, typically from an original source and using both human and technological means, for input into the Intelligence Cycle for the purpose of meeting a defined tactical or strategic intelligence goal.

Collection Plan

the preliminary step toward completing an assessment of intelligence requirements to determine what type of information needs to be collected, alternatives for how to collect the information, and a timeline for collecting information.

Command and Control

command and control functions are performed through an arrangement of personnel, equipment, communications, facilities and procedures employed by a commander in planning directing, coordinating, and controlling forces and operations in the accomplishment of a mission.

Commodity (Illegal)
(Criminal Intelligence)

any item or substance that is inherently unlawful to possess (contraband) or materials which, if not contraband, are themselves being distributed, transacted, or marketed in an unlawful manner.

Commodity Flow Analysis

graphic depictions and descriptions of transactions, shipment, and distribution of contraband goods and money derived from unlawful activities in order to aid in the disruption of the unlawful activities and apprehend those persons involved in all aspects of the unlawful activities.

Common Law Court Movement

adherents to the Common Law Court Movement declare themselves exempt from the laws of the United States. Using pseudo-legal theories based on selective interpretations of the Bible, the Magna Carta, state and federal court decisions, and the U.S. and state constitutions. These activists present a serious threat to the rule of law by using phone liens, money orders and documents in an attempt to defy the authority of legitimate courts.

Common Terrorism Information Sharing
Standards (CTISS)
(Criminal Intelligence)

business process-driven, performance based "common standards" for preparing terrorism information for maximum distribution and access, to enable the acquisition, access, retention, production, use, management, and sharing of terrorism information within the ISE. Two categories of common standards are formally identified under CTISS: functional standards and technical standards. Functional standards set forth rules, conditions, and characteristics of data and mission products supporting, ISE business process areas. Technical standards document specific technical methodologies and practices to design and implement information sharing capability into ISE systems. CTISS, such as ISE-SAR, are implemented in ISE participant infrastructures that include ISE Shared Spaces as described the *ISE Enterprise Architecture Framework*.

Communications Intelligence (COMINT)

the capture of information, either encrypted or in "plaintext," exchanged between intelligence targets or transmitted by a known or suspected intelligence target for the purposes of tracking communications patterns and protocols (traffic analysis), establishing links between intercommunicating parties or groups, and/or analysis of the substantive meaning of the communications.

Compartmentation

(1) Formal system of restricted access to intelligence activities, such systems established by and/or managed under the cognizance of the DCI to protect the sensitive aspects of sources, methods, and analytical procedures of foreign intelligence information, limited to individuals with a specific need for such information and who are therefore given special security clearances and indoctrination in order to have access to it all.

(2) Establishment and management of an intelligence organization, or activities of one component is made available to another component or individual only to the extent required for the performance of assigned duties.

Computer security
(Criminal Intelligence)

the protection of information through the use of technology, processes, and training.

Conclusion
(Criminal Intelligence)

a definitive statement about a suspect, action or state of nature based on the analysis of information.

Confidential Classification

applies to information, the unauthorized disclosure of which reasonably could be expected to cause damage to the national security that the original classification authority is able to identify or describe.

Confidentiality
(Criminal Intelligence)

closely related to privacy but is not identical. It refers to the obligations of individuals and institutions to use information under their control appropriately once it has been disclosed to them. One observes rules of confidentiality out of respect for and to protect and preserve the privacy of others.

Contagion Theory

the spread of a behavior pattern from person to person or group to group through suggestion, propaganda, rumor, or imitation. The theory states that terrorists will copy prior successful attacks, which will result in an ever-increasing rate of terrorist activity.

Continuing Criminal Enterprise

any individual, partnership, corporation, association, or other legal entity and any union or group of individuals associated in fact, although not a legal entity, that are involved in a continuing or perpetuating criminal activity.

Continuing Criminal Enterprise
(Criminal Intelligence)

any individual, partnership, corporation, association, or other legal entity and any union or group of individuals associated in fact, although not a legal entity, that are involved in continuing or perpetuating criminal activity.

Coordination
(Criminal Intelligence)

the process of interrelating work functions, responsibilities, duties, resources, and initiatives directed toward goal attainment.

Counterintelligence

is "Information gathered and activities conducted to protect against espionage, other intelligence activities, sabotage, or assassinations conducted by or on behalf of foreign governments or elements thereof, foreign organizations, or foreign persons or international terrorist activities." One type of intelligence included in the "National Intelligence" or "intelligence related to National Security" definitions. (50 U.S.C. 401a; Section 3 of the National Security Act of 1947, as amended.)

Counterintelligence (alternative definition)

information gathered, and activities conducted, to protect against espionage, other intelligence activities, sabotage, or assassinations conducted by or on behalf of foreign organizations, or foreign persons, or international terrorist activities.

Counterintelligence
(Criminal Intelligence)

information compiled, analyzed, and/or disseminated in an effort to investigate espionage, sedition, or subversion that is related to national security concerns. It also is defined as a national security intelligence activity that involves blocking or developing a strategic response to other groups, governments, or individuals through the identification, neutralization, and manipulation of their intelligence services.

Countermeasure (short definition)

an action taken or physical entity principally used to reduce or eliminate one or more vulnerabilities.

Countermeasure (long definition)

an action taken or a physical capability provided whose principal purpose is to reduce or eliminate one or more vulnerabilities or to reduce the probability of an attack. The countermeasures may also affect the intent and/or capability of the threats, and may affect the asset's value. The costs of a countermeasure may include indirect costs such as reduced operational effectiveness, adverse publicity, unfavorable working conditions, and political consequences. Countermeasures are intended to reduce the probability that an attack will occur, or, if an attack does occur, to reduce the probability that the attack will succeed in causing a failure or significant damage. In contrast, consequences mitigation features, actions and strategies are intended to limit the impacts (consequences) of a failure that occurs as a result of an attack.

Counterterrorism

Offensive measures taken to prevent, deter, and respond to a terrorist action or the documented threat of such an act. Counterterrorism is often responsive or reactive to terror threats or attacks. It entails using "active measures" which incorporate the direct intervention of terrorist groups or the targeting of terrorist personnel.

Controlled Unclassified Information (CUI)

"A categorical designation that refers to unclassified information that does not meet the standards for National Security Classification under Executive Order 12958, as amended, but is (i) pertinent to national interests of the United States or to important interests of entities outside the federal government, and (ii) under law or policy requires protection from unauthorized disclosure, special handling safeguards, or prescribed limits on exchange or dissemination. Henceforth, the designation CUI replaces "Sensitive But Unclassified" (SBU)," (Presidential Memorandum to Heads of Executive Departments and Agencies, Designation and Sharing of Controlled Unclassified [CUI], May 7, 2008.)

Controlled Unclassified Information (CUI)
Framework and Implementation

refers to the single set of policies and procedures governing the designation, making, safeguarding, and dissemination of CUI terrorism-related information that originates in departments and agencies, regardless of the medium used for the display, storage, or transmittal of such information. The President's May 7, 2008, Memorandum directed all federal agencies to implement the CUI Framework, which consists of policies and standards for the designation, making, safeguarding, and dissemination of any CUI terrorism-related information within the ISE that originates in federal agencies, regardless of the medium used for its display, storage, or transmittal. The President designated the National Archives and Records Administration (NARA) as the Executive Agent responsible for overseeing and managing implementation of the framework, to include the development of CUI policy standards and implementation guidance. Implementation is expected to occur over a 5-year transition period. The Memorandum designates that all CUI shall merit one of two levels of safeguarding procedures standard (marked "Controlled") or enhanced (marked "Controlled Enhanced") and one of two levels of dissemination controls "Standard Dissemination" or "Specified Dissemination." This allows for three combinations of safeguarding procedures and dissemination controls:

"Controlled with Standard Dissemination"
meaning the information requires standard safeguarding measures that reduce the risks of unauthorized or inadvertent disclosure. Dissemination is permitted to the extent that it is reasonably believed that it would further the execution of a lawful or official purpose.

"Controlled with Specified Dissemination"
meaning the information requires safeguarding measures that reduce the risks of unauthorized or inadvertent disclosure. Material contains additional instruction on what dissemination is permitted.

"Controlled Enhanced with Specified Dissemination"
meaning the information requires safeguarding measures more stringent than those normally required once the inadvertent or unauthorized disclosure would create risk of substantial harm. Material contains additional instructions on what dissemination is permitted.

With regards to the CUI Framework's application to state, local, tribal, and private sector entities:

- The CUI Memorandum applies only to federal Executive Branch departments and agencies that handle and share terrorism-related information or are participants in the information Sharing Environment.

- State and local government officials participated extensively in developing the framework, and many have indicated that they will voluntarily adopt CUI Framework.

The President directed NARA to develop and issue CUI policy standards and implementation guidance consistent with the Memorandum, to include appropriate recommendations for state, local, tribal, private sector, and foreign partner entities for implementing the CUI Framework.

The Memorandum directs that federal agencies receiving CUI which originated from a state, local, tribal, private sector, or foreign partner shall retain any nonfederal legacy markings, unless the originator authorizes its removal.

The information Sharing Council's State, Local, tribal, and Private Sector Subcommittee will be consulted during the development of procedures, guidelines, and standards necessary to establish, implement, and maintain the CUI Framework. (Presidential Memorandum to Heads of Executive Departments and Agencies, Designation, and Sharing of Controlled Unclassified Information [CUI, May 7, 2008.)

Coordination

the process of interrelating work functions, responsibilities, duties, resources, and initiatives directed toward goal attainment.

Covert Action

- An operation designed to influence governments, events, organizations, or persons in support of foreign policy in a manner that is not necessarily attributed to the sponsoring power; it may include political, economic, or paramilitary activities.

- Operations that are so planned and executed as to conceal the identity of, or permit plausible deniability by, the sponsor.

Covert Intelligence

a covert activity is planned and executed to conceal the collection of information and/or the identity of any officer or agent participating in the activity.

Covert Operation

preferred term

Clandestine Operation.

A covert operation encompassing covert action and clandestine collection.

Credentials
(Criminal Intelligence)

information that includes identification and proof of identification that is used to gain access to local and network resources. Examples of credentials are user names, passwords, smart cards, and certificates.

Crime Analysis
(Criminal Intelligence)

the process of analyzing information collected on crimes and police service delivery variables in order to give direction for police officer deployment, resource allocation, and policing strategies as a means to maximize crime prevention activities and the cost-effective operation of the police department.

Crime Pattern Analysis (Criminal Intelligence)

an assessment of the nature, extent, and changes of crime based on the characteristics of the criminal incident, including modus operandi, temporal, and geographic variables.

Criminal History Record Information (CHRI) (Criminal Intelligence)

Information collected by criminal justice agencies on individuals, consisting of identifiable descriptions and notations of arrests, detentions, indictments, information, or other formal criminal charges and any disposition arising therefrom, including sentencing, correctional supervision, and/or release. The term does not include identification, such as fingerprint records, to the extent that such information does not indicate involvement of the individual in the criminal justice system.

Criminal Intelligence

the product of the analysis of raw information related to crimes or crime patterns with respect to an identifiable person or group of persons in an effort to anticipate, prevent, or monitor possible criminal activity.

Criminal Intelligence (alternative definition)

the end product (output) of an analytic process that collects and assesses information about crimes and/or criminal enterprises with the purpose of making judgments and inferences about community conditions, potential problems, and criminal activity with the intent to pursue criminal prosecution or project crime trends or support informed decision-making by management.

Criminal Intelligence Information (Criminal Intelligence)

information deemed relevant to the identification of and the criminal activity engaged in by an individual or organization that is reasonably suspected of involvement in criminal activity. Criminal intelligence reports are records that are maintained in a criminal intelligence system per 28 CFR Part 23 (FBI).

Criminal Investigative Analysis (Criminal Intelligence)

an analytic process that studies serial offenders, victims, and crime scenes in order to assess characteristics and behaviors of offender(s) with the intent to identify or aid in the identification of the offender(s).

Criminal Predicate

information about an individual or his/her behavior that may only be collected and stored in a law enforcement intelligence records system when there is reasonable suspicion that the individual is involved in criminal conduct or activity and the information is relevant to that criminal conduct or activity.

Critical Asset

an asset that supports national security, national economic security, and/or crucial public health and safety activities.

Critical Infrastructure

physical or cyber-based system essential to the minimum operations of the economy and government.

Critical Infrastructures (alternative definition)

those systems and assets, both physical and cyber, so vital to the nation that their incapacity or destruction would have a debilitating effect on national security, national economic security, and/or national public health and safety.

Critical Infrastructure (Criminal Intelligence)

certain national infrastructures that are so vital that their incapacity or destruction would have debilitating impact on the defense or economic security of the United States. These critical infrastructures are:

- Telecommunications

- Electrical power grids

- Gas and oil storage and transportation

- Banking and finance
- Transportation
- Water supply systems
- Emergency services (including medical, police, fires, and rescue
- Continuity of government

Criticality Assessment

is a process designed to systematically identify and evaluate important assets and infrastructure in terms of various factors, such as the mission and significance of a target.

Cryptanalysis

the process of deciphering encrypted communications of an intelligence target.

Cryptography

the creation of a communications code/encryption system for communication transmission with the intent of precluding the consumption and interpretation of the communications by an unauthorized or unintended party.

**Cryptology
(Criminal Intelligence)**

the study of communications encryption methods that deal with the development of "codes" and the "scrambling" of communications to prevent an unauthorized or unintended party from intercepting the communications.

Cyberterrorism

is defined by the U.S. government as "a criminal act perpetrated through computers resulting in violence, death and/or destruction, and creating terror for the purpose of coercing a government to change its policies" or "politically motivated use of computers as weapons as or as target, by sub-national groups or clandestine agents intent on violence, to influence an audience or cause a government to change its policies."

D

DAISH

DAISH is an acronym [Arabic: Al-Dawlah Al-Islamiyah fe Al-Iraq wa Al-Sham] or the ISIL (the so-called Islamic State of Iraq and the Levant). DAISH has a pejorative tone to it taking away some of ISIL's credibility because it does not give them the status of being a state. France and Iraq no longer use ISIL, and instead use DAISH. Much of the Arab world refers to ISIL as DAISH. (also spelled DAESH)

Data Breach
(Criminal Intelligence)

the unintentional release of secure information to an untrusted environment. This may include incidents such as theft or loss of digital media, including computer tapes, hard drives, or laptop computers containing such media upon which such information is stored unencrypted; posted such information on the World Wide Web or on a computer otherwise accessible from the Internet without proper information security precautions; transfer of such information to a system that is not completely open but is not appropriately or formally accredited for security at the approved level, such as unencrypted e-mail; or transfer of such information to the information system of a possibly hostile agency or environment where it may be exposed to more intensive decryption techniques.

Data Protection
(Criminal Intelligence)

encompasses the range of legal, regulatory, and institutional mechanisms that guide the collection, use protection, and disclosure of information.

Data Element

a field within a database that describes or defines a specific characteristic or attribute.

Data Owner

the agency that originally enters information or data into a law enforcement records system.

Data Quality
(Criminal Intelligence)

controls implemented to ensure that all information in a law enforcement agency's records system is complete, accurate, and secure.

Deconfliction
(Criminal Intelligence)

the process or system used to determine whether multiple law enforcement agencies are investigating the same person or crime and which provides notification to each agency involved of the shared interest in the case, as well as providing contact information. This is an information and intelligence sharing process that seeks to minimize conflicts between agencies and maximize the effectiveness of an investigation.

Deductive Logic

the reasoning process of taking information and arriving at conclusions from within that information.

de facto

exercising power as if legally constituted.

Defense Intelligence Agency (DIA)

is an agency of the Intelligence Community responsible for satisfying the foreign military and military-related intelligence requirements of the Secretary of Defense, the Joint Chiefs of Staff, the unified and Specified Commands, and other Defense components, and, as appropriate, non-defense agencies. It is a provider of military intelligence for national foreign intelligence and counterintelligence products and is responsible for coordinating the intelligence activities of the military services and managing the Defense Attaché System.

de jure

by right; rightfully; legal; of right.

Deployment
(Criminal Intelligence)

the short-term assignment of personnel to address specific crime problems or police service demands.

Designated State and/or Major Urban Area
Fusion Center
(Criminal Intelligence)

the fusion center in each state designated as the primary or lead fusion center for the information-sharing environment.

Detection

A countermeasure strategy that is intended to identify an adversary attempting to attack an asset or exploit an asset's vulnerability, in order to provide real time observation as well as post-incident analysis of the activities and identity of the adversary.

Deterrence

A countermeasure strategy that is intended to prevent or discourage the occurrence of a threat by means of fear or doubt. Physical *security* systems such as warning signs, lights, uniform guards, cameras, metal bars are examples of countermeasures that provide deterrence.

Direct Action

is a term used to describe a wide array of protest actions and confrontation methods, including both non-violent techniques, such as boycotts or sit-ins, and violent actions like sabotage or guerrilla warfare. The term is often used by political groups pursuing increased militancy. Many environmental extremist groups practice illegal direct action. The term was also the name of a famous French terrorist group active in the 1980s: Action Directe.

Dirty Bomb

another name for a radiological device. Also known as a "radiological dispersal device (RDD)," combines conventional explosives with radioactive materials in an effort to spread the potentially harmful material over a large distance. Often called a "weapon of mass destruction," most experts believe that the actual threat from radioactive material would be low, with conventional explosives (and resultant panic caused by the bomb) posing a larger threat.

Disclosure
(Criminal Intelligence)

the release, transfer, provision of access to, sharing, publication, or divulging of personal information in any manner electronic, verbal, or in writing to an individual, agency, or organization outside the agency that collected it. Disclosure is an aspect of privacy, focusing on information that may be available only to certain people for certain purposes but which is not available to everyone.

Disinformation

false information about a country's military strength or plans, publicly announced or planted in the news media, especially in other countries.

Dissemination (of Intelligence)

the process of effectively distributing analyzed intelligence utilizing certain protocols in the most appropriate format to those in need of the information to facilitate their accomplishment of organizational goals.

Domestic Collection

the acquisition of foreign intelligence information within the United States from governmental or nongovernmental organizations or individuals who are witting sources and choose to cooperate by sharing such information.

Domestic terrorism

incidents perpetrated by local nationals against a purely domestic target.

double entendre

ambiguity of meaning arising from language that lends itself to more than one interpretation; a word or expression capable of two interpretations one of which has a risqué connotation.

Due Diligence
(Criminal law)

in criminal law, due diligence is the only available defense to a crime that is one of strict liability (i.e., a crime that only requires an *actus reus* and no *mens rea*). Once the criminal offense is proven, the defendant must prove on balance that they did everything possible to prevent the act from happening. It is not enough that they took the normal standard of care in their industry – they must show that they took every reasonable precaution.

Due Diligence

is also used in criminal law to describe the scope of the duty of a prosecutor, to take efforts to turn over potentially exculpatory evidence, to (accused) criminal defendants.

Due Process
(Criminal Intelligence)

fundamental fairness during the course of the criminal justice process, including adherence to legal standards and the civil rights of the police constituency; the adherence to principles that are fundamental to justice.

E

El Paso Intelligence Center (EPIC)

a cooperative intelligence center serving as a clearinghouse and intelligence resource for local, state, and federal law enforcement agencies. Its primary concern is drug trafficking; however, intelligence on other crimes is also managed by EPIC.

Electronically maintained (Criminal Intelligence)

information stored by a computer or on an electronic medium from which the information may be retrieved by a computer, such as electronic memory chips, magnetic tape, magnetic disk, or compact disc optical media.

Electronically transmitted (Criminal Intelligence)

information exchanged with a computer using electronic media, such as the movement of information from one location to another by magnetic or optical media, or transmission over the Internet, intranet, extranet, leased lines, dial-up lines, private networks, telephone voices response, or faxback systems. It does not include faxes, telephone calls, video teleconferencing, or messages left on voicemail.

Enterprise
(Criminal Intelligence)

any individual, partnership, corporation, association, or other legal entity and any union or group of individuals associated in fact, although not a legal entity.

Environmental/Animal Rights

terrorists commit acts of terrorism to influence their government's environmental policy or to stop private sector actions that are perceived to be harmful to a region's ecology and wildlife or animals in general.

Estimate

(1) An analysis of a foreign situation, development, or trend that identifies its major elements and interprets the significance, and appraises the future possibilities and the prospective results of the various actions that might be taken.

(2) An appraisal of the capabilities, vulnerabilities, and potential courses of action of a foreign nation or combination of nations in consequences of a specific national plan, policy, decision, or contemplated course of action.

(3) An analysis of an actual or contemplated clandestine operation in relation to the situation in which it is or would be conducted in order to identify and appraise

such factors as available and needed assets, and potential obstacles, accomplishments, and consequences.

Evaluation (of Information)
(Criminal Intelligence)

review of all information collected for the intelligence cycle for its quality, with an assessment of the validity and reliability of the information.

Event Flow Analysis
(Criminal Intelligence)

graphic depictions and descriptions of incidents, behaviors, and people involved in an unlawful event, intended to help understand how an event occurred as a tool to aid in prosecution as well as prevention of future unlawful events.

Exemptions (to the Freedom of Information Act)
(Criminal Intelligence)

circumstances wherein a law enforcement agency is not required to disclose information from a Freedom of Information Act (FOIA) request.

ex officio

by virtue of, because of an office.

Extortion

the act of requisitioning money, supplies, or manpower without authority or compensation. Extortion is a common source of funding for many terrorist groups.

Extortion can occur in many forms. Violent groups can use the threat to force 'tax' populations.

F

fait accompli

accomplished fact

FIP (Fair Information Principles) (Criminal Intelligence)

The Fair Information Principles (FIPs) are contained within the Organization for Economic Co-operation and Development's (OECD) *Guidelines for Economic Co-operation on the Protection of Privacy and Transborder Flows of Personal Data.* These were developed around commercial transactions and the transborder exchange of information; however, they do provide a straightforward description of underlying privacy and information exchange principles and provide a simple framework for the legal analysis that need to be done with regard to privacy in integrated justice systems. Some of the individual principles may not apply in all instances of an integrated justice system. The eight FIPs are:

- Collection limitation principle

- Data quality principle

- Purpose specification principle

- Use limitation principle

- Security safeguards principle

- Openness principle

- Individual participation principle

- Accountability principle

Fascism

a specific form of right-wing authoritarianism based on a cult of personality of the leader. The fascist political model is based on Germany's Adolph Hitler and Italy's Benito Mussolini. Nationalism, which may sometimes include official racism, is a key element of fascism. Many right-wing terrorist groups use fascist ideals to shape their actions and goals.

Fatwa

in Islam, a declarative legal interpretation by a cleric or religious jurist that can often provide the basis for court decisions and even government actions. Certain Islamic extremists often use fatwas as justification for terrorist acts.

Fedayeen

an Arabic term meaning "those who sacrifice." Generally refers to irregular military units who operate using guerrilla or terrorist tactics.

FDIC

Federal Deposit Insurance Corporation

Federal Bureau of Investigation (FBI)

the FBI is within the Department of Justice. It is the principal law enforcement investigative arm of the U.S. government. It is a member of the Intelligence Community.

feng shui

the Chinese art or practice of creating harmonious surroundings that enhances the balance of yin and yang, as in arranging furniture or determining the location of a house.

Field Intelligence Group (FIG) (Criminal Intelligence)

the centralized intelligence component in a Federal Bureau of Investigation (FBI) field office that is responsible for the management, execution, and coordination of intelligence functions within the field office region or domain.

Field Intelligence Report (FIR) (Criminal Intelligence)

an officer-initiated interview of a person believed by the officer to be acting in a suspicious manner that may be indicative of planning or preparing to conduct criminal activity.

Financial Analysis

a review and analysis of financial data to ascertain the presence of criminal activity. It can include bank record analysis, net worth analysis, financial profiles, source and applications of funds, financial statement analysis, and/or Bank Secrecy Act record analysis. It can also show destinations of proceeds of crime and support prosecutions.

Financial Crime Enforcement Network (FinCEN)

FinCEN is a bureau of the Treasury Department that collects and analyzes information about financial transactions in order to combat domestic and international money laundering, terrorist financing, and other financial crimes.

Finished Intelligence

(1) The product resulting from the collection, processing, integration, analysis, evaluation, and interpretation of available information concerning foreign countries or areas.

(2) The final result of the production step of the intelligence cycle is the intelligence product.

Firewall
(Criminal Intelligence)

a security solution that segregates one portion of a network from another portion, allowing only authorized network traffic to pass through according to traffic-filtering rules.

FISA Court

Court that reviews, for sufficiency applications for orders issued under the Federal Intelligence Surveillance Act.

FISA Order

Order authorized under the Foreign Intelligence Surveillance Act to conduct electronic or physical searches within the U.S. for foreign intelligence purposes.

Fissionable Material

isotopes that can undergo nuclear fission, including those that cannot sustain a nuclear reaction when they fission.

Fissile Material

isotopes that can undergo a self-sustaining chain reaction nuclear fission. The only two fissile isotopes of note are uranium-235 and plutonium-239. All uranium contains some uranium-235; thus, all uranium is nuclear material.

Flow Analysis
(Criminal Intelligence)

the review of raw data to determine the sequence of events or interactions that may reflect criminal activity. It can include timelines, event flow analysis, commodity flow analysis, and activity flow analysis and may show missing actions or events that need further investigation.

For Official Use Only (FOUO)

a designation applied to unclassified sensitive information that may be exempt from mandatory release to the public under FOIA. This designation has been replaced by Controlled Unclassified Information (CUI) Framework. (Presidential Memorandum to Heads of Executive Departments and Agencies, Designation and Sharing of Controlled Unclassified Information (CUI), May 7, 2008.)

Forecast (as related to Criminal Intelligence)

the product of an analytic process that provides a probability of future crimes and crime patterns based upon a comprehensive, integrated analysis of past, current, and developing trends.

Foreign intelligence service

an organization of a foreign government that engages in intelligence activities.

Foreign Liaison

Efforts to work with foreign government intelligence services, including law enforcement agencies that gather or carry out intelligence-related activities. Examples of foreign liaison include sharing information, joint collection efforts, and the arrest of suspected terrorists by foreign governments using U.S.-supplied information. Every major U.S. intelligence agency has some form of liaison relationship with foreign governments.

Freedom of Information Act (FOIA)

the Freedom of Information Act, 5 U.S.C. 552, enacted in 1966, statutorily provides that any person has a right, enforceable in court, to access federal agency records, except, to the extent that such records (or portions thereof) are protected from disclosure by one of nine exemptions.

Fundamentalism

strict adherence to ancient or fundamental doctrines and texts, usually within a religion. Fundamentalism offers "no concessions to modern developments in thoughts or customs." (Oxford dictionary) Fundamentalist terrorism is usually associated with Islamic fundamentalists, who often seek to impose sacred Islamic law and and/or establish a pan-Arab or pan-Muslim theocratic empire known as a caliphate.

Fusion Center

an organized structure to coalesce data and information for the purpose of analyzing, linking and disseminating intelligence. Most often used to define a state-level intelligence organization. Also defined as a collaborative effort of two or more agencies that provide resources, expertise, and information to the center with the goal of maximizing the ability to detect, prevent, investigate and respond to criminal and terrorism activity (*Fusion Center Guidelines,* August, 2006); recognized as a valuable information sharing resource, state and major urban area fusion centers are the focus, but not exclusive points, within the state and local environment for the receipt and sharing of terrorism information, homeland security information, and law enforcement information related to terrorism. Federal agencies will provide terrorism-related information to state, local, and tribal authorities primarily through these fusion centers, which may further customize such information for dissemination to satisfy intra- or interstate needs. Likewise, fusion centers enable the effective communication of locally generated terrorism-related information to the federal government and other fusion centers through the ISE. (*National Strategy for Information Sharing,* October 2007.)

Fusion Center Guidelines, August 2006

A nationally recognized document developed to ensure that fusion centers are established and operated consistently, resulting in enhanced coordination efforts, strengthened partnerships, and improved crime-fighting and anti-terrorism capabilities. The guidelines were developed by law enforcement intelligence, public safety, and private sector subject-matter experts through the Global Justice Information Sharing Initiative and the Homeland Security Advisory Council. The Guidelines have been endorsed by the U.S. Department of Justice and Homeland Security and the *National Strategy for Information Sharing*.

Fusion Process

the overreaching process of managing the flow of information and intelligence across levels and sectors of government and private industry. It goes beyond establishing an information/intelligence center or creating computer network. The Fusion Process supports the implementation of risk-based, information-driven prevention, response, and consequence management programs. The Fusion Process turns information and intelligence into actionable knowledge. (*Fusion Center Guidelines,* August 2006.)

G

Gaming

an adaptive process of developing consequence mitigation strategies and countermeasures in response to changing threats, in recognition that threats will evolve over time.

General information or data (Criminal Intelligence)

information that may include records, documents, or files pertaining to law enforcement operations, such as computer-aided dispatch (CAD) data, incident data, and management information. Information that is maintained in a records management, CAD system, etc., for statistical/retrieval purposes. Information may be either resolved or unresolved. The record is maintained per statute, rule or policy.

Granularity (Criminal Intelligence)

considers the specific details and pieces of information, including nuances and situational inferences that constitute the elements on which intelligence is developed through analysis.

Green-Brown Alliance

any alliance between left-wing environmentalist and right-wing extremists.

Guerrilla (guerilla)

refers to a member of an irregular military force operating in small groups designed to constantly harass and combat a numerically superior enemy. Guerrilla warfare and tactics are often practiced by insurgents and terrorist groups.

H

habeas corpus

you should have the body; any of several common-law writs issued to bring a party before a court or judge.

Hacker

a person who has expertise and skills to penetrate computer systems and alter such systems, processes, and/or information/data in files but does not damage and commits no theft or crime. While a hacker may enter files or systems without authorization, the action is more akin to a trespass and no theft or damage results.

Hajj

is an annual Islamic pilgrimage to Mecca. One who makes that pilgrimage is called a mustati.

Hard target

is a target that has a significant security presence in order to deter a terrorist attack. Examples: military bases, airports, and government agencies.

Hawala

an underground banking system based on trust whereby money can be made available internationally without actually moving it or leaving a record of the transaction; terrorists make extensive use of hawala.

Hijacking

commandeering a vehicle (truck, train, car, plane, etc.) in transit in order to take control of it and use it for one's own purposes. This may include stealing the vehicle or cargo, kidnapping the passengers, traveling to a new destination, destroying the vehicle or using the vehicle as a weapon.

HPSCI

House Permanent Select Committee on Intelligence is a permanent select committee of the House of Representatives established by House Rule XLVIII, whose function is to monitor and provide oversight for the Intelligence Community and intelligence-related activities of all other government organizations. The committee is also responsible for legislation pertaining to intelligence agencies and activities, including authorizing appropriations for such activities.

Homeland Security Advisory System

an information and communication structure designed by the U.S. government for disseminating information to all levels of government and the American people regarding the risk of terrorist attacks and for providing a framework to assess the risk at five levels: Low, Guarded, Elevated, High, and Severe.

Homeland security information (Criminal Intelligence)

as defined in Section 892(f)(1) of the Homeland Security Act of 2002 and codified at 6 U.S.C. 482(f)(1), homeland security information means any information possessed by a federal, state, or local agency that (a) relates to a threat of terrorist activity; (b) relates to the ability to prevent, interdict, or disrupt terrorist activity; (c) would improve the identification of a suspected terrorist or terrorist organization; or (d) would improve the response to a terrorist act.

Homeland Security Intelligence (Criminal Intelligence)

the collection and analysis of information concerned with noncriminal domestic threats to critical infrastructure, community health, and public safety for the purpose of preventing the threat or mitigating the effects of the threat. (Same as All Hazards Intelligence).

Human Intelligence (HUMINT)

intelligence-gathering methods that require human interaction or observation of the target or targeted environment. The intelligence is collected through the use of one's direct senses or the optical and/or audio enhancement of the senses.

Hypothesis
(Criminal Intelligence)

an interim conclusion regarding persons, events, and/or commodities based on the accumulation and analysis of intelligence information that is to be proven or disproved by further investigation analysis.

I

Identification
(Criminal Intelligence)

a process whereby a real-world entity is recognized and its identity established. Identity is operationalized in the abstract world of information systems as a set of information about an entity that uniquely differentiates it from other similar entities. The set of information may be as small as a single code, specifically designed as an identifier, or a collection of data, such as a given and family name, date of birth, and address. An organization's identification process consists of the acquisition of the relevant identifying information.

Imagery

the representation of an object or locale produced on any medium by optical or electronic means. The nature of the image will be dependent on the sensing media and sensing platform.

Improvised Explosive Device (IED)

is a device placed or fabricated in an improvised manner incorporating destructive, lethal, noxious, pyrotechnic or incendiary chemicals, designed to destroy, disfigure, distract or harass. They may incorporate military stores or explosives, but are normally devised from non-military components. IEDs are similar to land mines, but are generally home-made and of varying explosive force. The term IED came to public use during the violent insurgency that followed the 2003 U.S.-led invasion of Iraq.

Indicator

generally defined and observable actions that, based on an analysis of past known behaviors and characteristics, collectively suggest that a person may be committing, may be preparing to commit, or has committed an unlawful act.

Individual responsibility (Criminal Intelligence)

because a privacy notice is not self-implementing, an individual within an organization's structure must also be assigned responsibility for enacting and implementing the notice.

Inductive Logic

the reasoning process of taking diverse pieces of specific information and inferring a broader meaning of the information through the course of hypothesis development.

Inference Development

the creation of probabilistic conclusion, estimate, or prediction related to an intelligence target based on the use of inductive or deductive logic in the analysis of raw information related to the target.

Informant
(Criminal Intelligence)

an individual not affiliated with a law enforcement agency who provides information about criminal behavior to a law enforcement agency. An informant may be a community member, a businessperson, or a criminal informant who seeks to protect him/herself from prosecution and/or provide the information in exchange for payment.

Information
(Criminal Intelligence)

includes any data about people, organizations, events, incidents, or objects, regardless of the medium in which it exists. Information, received by law enforcement agencies can be categorized into four general areas: general data, including investigative information; tips and leads data; suspicious activity reports; and criminal intelligence information.

Information Sharing Environment

a trusted partnership among all levels of government, the private sector, and foreign partners to detect, prevent, preempt, and mitigate the effects of terrorism against the territory, people, and interests of the United States of America. This partnership enables the trusted, secure, and appropriate exchange of terrorism information, in the first instance, across the five federal communities; to and from state, local, and tribal governments, foreign allies, and the private sector; and at all levels of security classification.

Information Sharing Environment (ISE) Suspicious Activity Report (SAR) (ISE-SAR) Criminal Intelligence

a SAR that has been determined, pursuant to a two-step process established in the ISE-SAR Functional Standard, to have a potential terrorism nexus (i.e. to be reasonably indicative of criminal activity associated with terrorism).

Information Sharing System (Criminal Intelligence)

an integrated and secure methodology, whether computerized or manual, designed to efficiently and effectively distribute critical information about offenders, crimes, and/or events in order to enhance prevention and apprehension activities by law enforcement.

Information System

an organized means, whether manual or electronic, of collecting, processing, storing, and retrieving information about individual entities for purposes of record and reference.

Information quality
(Criminal Intelligence)

refers to various aspects of the information; the accuracy and validity of the actual value of the data, data structure, and database/data repository design. Traditionally, the basic elements of information quality have been identified as accuracy, completeness, currency, reliability, and context/meaning. Today, information quality is being more fully described in multidimensional models, expanding conventional views of the topic including considerations of accessibility, security, and privacy.

Insurgents

individuals who try to overthrow a government from within; not necessarily committed to violence against noncombatants. Not always, but insurgents can be terrorists.

Intelligence

the product of adding value to information and data through analysis. Intelligence is created for a purpose. It is the process by which analysis is applied to information and data to inform policy-making, decision-making, including decisions regarding the allocation of resources, strategic decisions, operations and tactical decisions. Intelligence serves many purposes among which are the identification and elimination of threat sources, the investigation and resolution of threats, the identification and treatment of security risk, the elimination of threat sources, the mitigation of harm associated with risk preemption, response, preparation and operations related to threats and risks.

Intelligence Analyst

a professional position in which the incumbent is responsible for taking the varied facts, documentation of circumstances evidence, interviews, and any other material related to a crime and organizing them into a logical and related framework for the purposes of developing a criminal case, explaining a criminal phenomenon, describing crime and crime trends and/or preparing materials for court and prosecution, or arriving at an assessment of a crime problem or crime group.

Intelligence Assessment

a comprehensive report on an intelligence issue related to criminal or national security threats available to local, state, tribal, and federal intelligence agencies and law enforcement agencies.

Intelligence Bulletins
(Criminal Intelligence)

a finished intelligence product in article format that describes new developments and evolving trends. The Bulletins are usually unclassified (Sensitive But Unclassified SBU) and available for distribution to local, state, tribal and federal law enforcement agencies.

Intelligence Community

Those agencies of the U.S. government, including the military that have the responsibility of preventing breaches to U.S. national security and responding to national security threats. The list of Intelligence Community members is taken from the ODNI Web page.

- Office of the Director of National Intelligence
- Army Intelligence
- Central Intelligence Agency
- Coast Guard Intelligence
- Defense Intelligence Agency
- Department of Energy
- Department of Homeland Security
- Department of State
- Air Force Intelligence
- Department of the Treasury

- Drug Enforcement Administration

- Federal Bureau of Investigation

- Marine Corps Intelligence

- National Geospatial Intelligence Agency

- National Reconnaissance Office

- National Security Agency

- Navy Intelligence

Intelligence Cycle

the process by which information and data is collected, evaluated, stored, analyzed, and then produced or placed in some form for dissemination to the intelligence consumer for use. The cycle consists of consumer, collector, evaluation, analysis, production, dissemination, consumption, and back to the consumer.

Intelligence Estimate (Criminal Intelligence)

an appraisal, expressed in writing or orally, of available intelligence relating to a specific situation or condition with a view to determine the courses of action open to criminal offenders and terrorists and the order of probability of their adoption. Includes strategic projections on the economic, human, and/or quantitative criminal impact of the crime issue that is subject to analysis.

Intelligence Function
(Criminal Intelligence)

that activity within a law enforcement agency responsible for some aspect of law enforcement intelligence, whether collection, analysis, and/or dissemination.

Intelligence Gap

an unanswered question about a cyber, criminal, or national security issue or threat.

Intelligence Information Reports (IIR)

raw, unevaluated intelligence concerning "perishable" or time-limited information about criminal or national security issues. While the full IIR may be classified, local, state, and tribal law enforcement agencies will have access to sensitive but unclassified information in the report under the tear line.

Intelligence-Led policing (ILP)
(Criminal Intelligence)

a process for enhancing law enforcement agency effectiveness toward reducing crimes, protecting community assets, and preparing for responses. ILP provides law enforcement agencies with an organization framework to gather and use multisource information and intelligence to make timely and targeted strategic, operational, and tactical decisions. Also defined as the dynamic use of intelligence to guide operational law enforcement activities to targets, commodities, or threats for both tactical responses and strategic decision making for resource allocation and/or strategic responses.

Intelligence Mutual Aid Pact (IMAP)

a formal agreement between law enforcement agencies designed to expedite the process of sharing information in intelligence records.

Intelligence Officer
(Criminal Intelligence)

a law enforcement officer assigned to an agency's intelligence function for purposes of investigation, liaison, or other intelligence-related activity that requires or benefits from having a sworn officer perform the activity.

Intelligence Products
(Criminal Intelligence)

reports or documents that contain assessments, forecasts, associations, links, and other outputs from the analytic process that may be disseminated for use by law enforcement agencies for prevention of crimes, target hardening, apprehension of offenders, and prosecution.

Intelligence Report

- A product of the production step of the intelligence cycle;
- Military usage-A specific report of information, usually on a single item, made at any level of command in tactical operations and disseminated

as rapidly as possible in keeping with the
timeliness of the information.

Intelligence Mission
(Criminal Intelligence)

the role that the intelligence function of a law
enforcement agency fulfills in support of the overall
mission of the agency, it specifies in general language
what the function is intended to accomplish.

Intelligence Officer
(Criminal Intelligence)

a law enforcement officer assigned to an agency's
intelligence function for the purposes of investigation,
liaison, or other intelligence-related activity that requires
or benefits from having a sworn officer perform the
activity.

Intelligence Process
(Criminal Intelligence)

an organized process by which information is gathered,
assessed, and distributed in order to fulfill the goals of
the intelligence function. It is a method of performing
analytic activities and placing the analysis in a usable
form.

Intelligence Products
(Criminal Intelligence)

reports or documents that contain assessments,
forecasts, associations, links, and other outputs from the
analytic process that may be disseminated for use by law

enforcement agencies for the prevention of crimes, targets, hardening, apprehension of offenders, and prosecution.

Intelligence Records (Files)
(Criminal Intelligence)

stored information on the activities and associations of individuals, organizations, businesses, and groups who are suspected (reasonable suspicion) of being involved in the actual or attempted planning, organizing, financing, or commissioning of criminal acts or are suspected of being or having been involved in criminal activities with known or suspected crime figures.

Intelligence Records Guidelines
(Criminal Intelligence)

derived from federal regulations 28 CFR Part 23, these are guidelines/standards for the development of records management policies and procedures used by law enforcement agencies.

Intelligence Requirement

a subject, general or specific, upon which there is a need for collection of intelligence information or the production of intelligence.

Intelligence-Led Policing
(Criminal Intelligence)

the dynamic use of intelligence to guide operational law enforcement activities to targets, commodities, or threats for both tactical responses and strategic decision making for resource allocation and/or strategic responses.

Intelligence Mutual Aid Pact (IMAP)

a formal agreement between law enforcement agencies designed to expedite the process of sharing information in intelligence records.

International Criminal Police Organization (INTERPOL)

a worldwide law enforcement organization established for mutual assistance in the prevention, detection, and deterrence of international crimes. It houses international police databases, provides secure international communications between member countries for the exchange of routine criminal investigative information, and is an information clearinghouse on international criminals/fugitives and stolen properties.

International Terrorism

terrorist acts that transcend national boundaries in their conduct or purpose, the nationalities of the victims, or the resolution of the incident. Such an act is usually designed to attract wide publicity to focus attention on the existence, cause, or demands of the perpetrators.

Intifada

literally means "shaking off" in Arabic or "inspiring." The term is commonly used when referring to Palestinian uprising against Israeli rule. It is generally accepted that there have been two Intifadas, the first beginning in 1987 and ending in 1993, and the second beginning in 2000, also known as the "al-Aqsa Intifada."

Invasion of privacy (Criminal Intelligence)

intrusion on one's solitude or into one's private affairs, public disclosure of embarrassing private information, publicity that puts one in a false light to the public, or appropriation of one's name or picture for personal or commercial advantage.

in absentia

in absence.

in toto

totally, entirely.

Investigatory Value (Criminal Intelligence)

Intelligence or information that is disseminated in the law enforcement community for surveillance, apprehension, or furtherance of an investigation.

ISE Shared Spaces Concept or Shared Spaces

The ISE Shared Spaces concept is a key element of the *ISE Enterprise Architecture Framework* and helps resolve the information-processing and usage problems identified by the 9/11 Commission. ISE Shared Spaces are networked data and information repositories used by ISE participants to make their standardized terrorism-related information, applications, and services accessible to other ISE participants. ISE Shared Spaces also provide an infrastructure solution for those ISE participants with national security system (NSS) network assets, historically sequestered with only other NSS systems, to interface with ISE participants having only civil networks assets. Additionally, ISE Shared Spaces also provide the means for foreign partners to interface and share terrorism information with their U.S. counterparts. For more information about the ISE Shared Spaces concept, reference the *ISE Enterprise Architecture Framework* and the *ISE Profile Architecture and Implementation Strategy* at www.ise.gov.

ISE-Suspicious Activity Report (ISE-SAR)

an ISE-SAR is a SAR that has been determined, pursuant to a two-piece process, to have a potential terrorism nexus. ISE-SAR business rules will serve as a unified process to support the reporting, tracking, processing, storage, and retrieval of terrorism-related suspicious activity reports across the ISE.

Islamic

is the adjective for Islam, which is the monotheistic religion, characterized by the acceptance of the doctrine of submission to Allah and to Muhammad as the chief and last prophet of Allah.

Islamists

is an adherent of an Islamic revivalist movement; often characterized by moral conservatism, literalism, and the attempt to implement Islamic values in all spheres of life; seeks to implement Islamic law and rejects the separation of religion and state.

J

Jaish

literally means "army" in Arabic. The term is often part of the name of many Middle Eastern and South Asian terrorist groups.

Jihad

striving on behalf of Islam; struggling to be a better Muslim. Examples of jihad are proselytizing and military action.

Jihadists

those committed to violence on behalf of Islam; are usually individuals from abroad who join an insurgency for religious reasons or to defend and propagate Islam. The IC has moved to using the term jihadist because referring to Islamic fighters as mujahadin (warriors) might convey more respect than is intended.

Joint Terrorism Task Force (JTFE)

the joint operational group, led by the FBI, that leverages the collective resources of member agencies to prevent, investigate, disrupt and deter terrorism threats that affect United States interests and facilities information sharing among partner agencies.

K

Kafir (kaffir)

indicates a nonbeliever in Allah; a person who hides, denies, or covers the truth; is similar to the term *infidel* in English. (NOTE: Kafir is a derogatory term used in South Africa. Kafir should not be used in finished intelligence.)

Key Asset

a person, an organization, group of organizations, system, or group of systems, the loss of which would have widespread and dire strategic, economic or social impact.

Key Resource
(Criminal Intelligence)

publicly or privately controlled resources essential to the minimal operations of the economy and government.

Key Word In Context (KWIC)
(Criminal Intelligence)

an automated system that indexes selected key words that represent the evidence or information being stored.

L

laissez-faire

a doctrine opposing governmental interference in economic affairs beyond the minimum necessary for the maintenance of peace and property rights.

Lashkar

literally means "battalion" in Urdu, the term is often part of the name of many Asian terrorist groups.

Law enforcement information (Criminal Intelligence)

any information obtained by or of interest to a law enforcement agency or official that is both (a) related to terrorism or the security of our homeland and (b) relevant to a law enforcement mission, including but not limited to information pertaining to an actual or potential criminal, civil, or administrative investigation or a foreign intelligence, counterintelligence , or counterterrorism investigation; assessment of or response to criminal threats and vulnerabilities; the existence, organization, capabilities, plans, intentions, vulnerabilities, means, methods, or activities of individuals or groups involved or suspected of involvement in criminal or unlawful conduct or assisting or associated with criminal or unlawful conduct; the existence, identification, detection, prevention, interdiction, or disruption of or response to criminal acts and violations of the law; identification, apprehension, prosecution, release, detention, adjudication, supervision, or rehabilitation of accused persons or criminal offenders; and victim/witness assistance.

Law Enforcement Intelligence LAWINT Criminal Intelligence)

the end product (output) of an analytic process that collects and assesses information about crimes and/or criminal enterprises with the purpose of making judgments and inferences about community conditions, potential problems, and criminal activity with the intent to pursue criminal prosecution or project crime trends or support informed decision making by management.

Law Enforcement Sensitive (Criminal Intelligence)

sensitive but unclassified information compiled for law enforcement purposes that if not protected from unauthorized access could reasonably be expected to (1) interfere with law enforcement proceedings, (2) deprive a person of a right to a fair trial or impartial adjudication, (3) constitute an unwarranted invasion of the personal privacy of others (4) disclose the identity of a confidential source, (5) disclose investigative techniques and procedures, and/or (6) endanger the life or physical safety of an individual.

**Lawful permanent resident
(Criminal Intelligence)**

a foreign national who has been granted the privilege of permanently living and working in the United States.

**Least privilege administration
(Criminal Intelligence)**

a recommended security practice in which every user is provided with only the minimum privileges needed to accomplish the tasks he or she is authorized to perform.

Leninism

the political and economic theories of Russian Marxist revolutionary Vladimir Lenin. Lenin modified Marxism by stressing that imperialism is the highest form of capitalism, shifting the class struggle from the developed world (as envisioned by Marx) to the developing world. Lenin also stressed that socialism in some countries was possible without worldwide revolution. In Soviet economic and political jargon, the term Marxism-Leninism was generally applied to the socialism practiced in the USSR and its satellite countries. Throughout history, many left-wing terrorist groups have used Leninist theories to justify terrorist attacks.

Logs
(Criminal Intelligence)

a necessary part of an adequate security system because they are needed to ensure that data is properly tracked and that only authorized individuals are getting access to the data.

Lone Wolf

an individual terrorist taking action without a leader or hierarchy. Also referred to as a Berserker.

M

Madrassa

Islamic religious or Koranic school. The term madrassa commonly refers to an Islamic religious school in which young children are educated in Islamic law and holy texts. There are tens of thousands of madrassas throughout the Middle East and South Asia, with an estimated 12,000 to 15,000 in Pakistan alone. Madrassas have become controversial, being accused of brainwashing children and preaching a form of strict Islam that encourages violence and terrorism against non-believers.

Maintenance of information (Criminal Intelligence)

applies to all forms of information storage. This includes electronic systems (for example databases) and non-electronic storage systems (for example, filing cabinets). To meet access requirements, an organization is not required to create new systems to maintain information or to maintain information beyond a time when it no longer serves an organization's purpose.

Malicious Software (MALWARE)

self-contained yet interactive computer programs that, when introduced into a computer can cause loss of memory, loss of data, or cause erroneous instructions to be given a computer program.

mano a mano

direct confrontation or conflict; head-on competition; a duel.

Maoism

The application of Marxism-Leninism to China by Mao Tse Tung. There is no specific addition to Communist theory that classifies it as Maoism. The term was introduced to raise the status of Mao to that of other great communist thinkers. It was often used pejoratively by other (Soviet) communists after the Sino-Soviet split. Mao's chief contribution to class struggle was theory on insurgent warfare. In *On Guerrilla Warfare*, he emphasized the importance of winning the support of the population and slowly growing an insurgency until it is powerful enough to take on the government's forces. There have been several terrorist groups throughout history that have employed Maoist theories both in their ideology and in the justification of violent action.

Marxism

the political and economic philosophy of Karl Marx and Friedrich Engels in which the relationship between capital and labor is the driving force behind social and political development in human history. Societies evolve in four states, culminating in a "worker's revolution." Terrorist groups waging "class struggle" in the name of Marxism appear in many parts of the world, including Latin America and Southeast Asia.

Metadata
(Criminal Intelligence)

in its simplest form, metadata is information (data) about information, more specifically information about a particular aspect of the collected information. An item or a metadata may describe an individual content item or a collection of content items. Metadata is used to facilitate the understanding, use, and management of information. The metadata required for this will vary based on the type of information and the context of use.

Methods
(Criminal Intelligence)

these are the methodologies (e.g., electronic surveillance or undercover operations) used to obtain and record information.

MI-6 (Military Intelligence, Section 6)

The British Secret Intelligence Service or SIS, which concentrates on foreign intelligence gathering on all subjects related to British national security.

Micro-Intelligence
(Criminal Intelligence)

intelligence activities focusing on current problems and crimes for either case development or resource allocation.

Misinformation

false or misleading information. (Unlike disinformation, there is no implied intention to deceive.)

modus operandi

a method of procedure.

modus vivendi

a feasible arrangement or practical compromise.

Money laundering

the practice of using multiple unlawful transactions of money and/or negotiable instruments gained through illegal activities with the intent of hiding the origin of the income, those who have been "paid" from the income, and/or the location of the unlawful income.

Mujahadin (NCTC preferred spelling)

literally means soldiers or warriors in a jihad. The term was first commonly used in reference to those who fought against the Soviet Union in Afghanistan.

N

National Central Bureau (NCB or USNCB)
(Criminal Intelligence)

in the United States, NCB headquarters (INTERPOL) is located in Washington, D.C.

National Criminal Intelligence Resource Center
(NCIRC)
(Criminal Intelligence)

an Internet Web site that contains information regarding law enforcement intelligence operations and practice and provides criminal justice professionals with a centralized resource information bank to access a multitude of criminal intelligence resources to help law enforcement agencies develop, implement, and retain a lawful and effective intelligence capacity.

National Criminal Intelligence Sharing Plan
(NCISP)
(Criminal Intelligence)

a formal intelligence sharing initiative, supported by the U.S. Department of Justice, Office of Justice Programs, that securely links local, state, tribal, and federal law enforcement agencies, facilitating the exchange of critical intelligence information. The Plan contains model policies and standards and is a blueprint for law enforcement administrators to follow when enhancing or building an intelligence function. It describes a nationwide communications capability that will link all levels of law enforcement personnel, including officers on the street, intelligence analysts, unit commanders, and police executives.

National Information Exchange Model (NIEM) (Criminal Intelligence)

a joint technical and functional standards program initiated by the U.S. Department of Homeland Security (DNS) and the U.S. Department of Justice (DOJ) that supports national-level interoperable information sharing.

National Intelligence or Intelligence Related to National Security

defined by Section 3 of the National Security Act of 1947, as amended, as "A) information relating to the capabilities intentions or activities of foreign governments or elements thereof, foreign organizations, or foreign persons, or international terrorist activities" (known as foreign intelligence); and B) "information gathered and activities conducted to protect against espionage, other intelligence activities, sabotage, or assassinations conducted by or on behalf of foreign governments or elements thereof, foreign organizations, or foreign persons, or international terrorist activities (known as "counterintelligence"), regardless of the source from which derived and including information gathered within or outside the United States, that (A) pertains to more than one United States Government agency; and (B) involves (i) threats to the United States, its people, property, or interests; (ii) the development, proliferation, or use of weapons of mass destruction; or (iii) any other matter bearing on the United States national or homeland security." (50 U.S.C. 401a) The goal of the National Intelligence effort to provide the President and the National Security Council with the necessary information on which to base decisions concerning the conduct and development of foreign, defense, and economic policy and the protection of United States national interests from foreign security threats. (Executive Order 12333.)

National Joint Terrorism Task Force

a joint entity led by the FBI and composed of over 40 agencies and established to enhance communication, coordination, and cooperation among federal, state, and local government agencies representing the intelligence, law enforcement, defense, diplomatic, public safety, and homeland security community by providing a point of fusion for the sharing of terrorism threats and intelligence; to provide operational support to the Counterterrorism Division; and to provide program management, oversight, and support for the JTTFs throughout the United States.

National Intelligence Board

(formerly the National Foreign Intelligence Board) is a body of senior U.S. intelligence community leaders led by the Director of National Intelligence (DNI). The Board is tasked with reviewing and approving National Intelligence Estimates (NIEs).

National Intelligence Council (NIC)

is comprised of the National Intelligence Officers (NIOs), their staff, and an analytic group. The NIOs support the DCI by producing national intelligence estimates and other interagency assessments and by advising him on the intelligence needs of policymakers.

National Intelligence Estimate (NIE)

- A thorough assessment of a situation in a foreign environment relevant to the formulation of foreign, economic, and national security policy, that projects probable future course of action and developments, and is structured to illuminate differences of view within the Intelligence Community; it is issued by the Director of National Intelligence with the advice of the National Intelligence Board;
- A strategic estimate of capabilities, vulnerabilities, produced at the national level as a composite of the views of the Intelligence Community.

National Intelligence Officer (NIO)

the senior staff officer assigned an area of functional or geographic responsibility. The NIO manages estimative and interagency intelligence production; he or she is the primary source of national-level substantive guidance to Intelligence Community planners, collectors and resource managers.

National Preparedness Guidelines

the U.S. government's guiding document for all-hazards preparedness, issued in October 2007. The *Guidelines* established a vision for national preparedness and provide a systematic approach for organizing, synchronizing, and prioritizing national (including federal, state, local, tribal, and territorial), efforts to strengthen national preparedness. The *Guidelines* are umbrella documents that collate many plans, strategies, and systems into an overarching framework, the National Preparedness System. The *Guidelines* were developed in response to the President's Homeland Security Presidential Directive 8 (HSPD-8) of December 17, 2003 (*"National Preparedness"*). The *Guidelines* adopt an all-hazards approach and facilitate a capability-based and risk-based investment planning process for preparedness.

National Security Agency (NSA)

is the Intelligence Community agency responsible for centralized coordination, direction, and performance of highly specialized technical functions in support of U.S. government activities to protect U.S. communications and produce foreign intelligence information. It coordinates, directs, and performs all cryptolotic functions for the U.S. government; collects, processes, and disseminates SIGINT information for DoD, national foreign intelligence, and counterintelligence purposes; and is the national executive agent for classified communications and computer security.

National Security Intelligence

the collection and analysis of information concerned with the relationship and equilibrium of the United States with foreign powers, organizations, and persons with regard to political and economic factors, as well as maintenance of the United States' sovereign principles.

Nationalist/Separatist

Nationalist terrorists see themselves as the representatives of their nation or national group. They commit acts of terrorism to defend what they believe to be the interests of their national group. Nationalist terrorist groups are often seeking statehood on behalf of a minority ethnic or religious group that is currently within a larger state, in which case the terrorists are separatists as well as nationalists.

Need to know
(Criminal Intelligence)

as a result of jurisdictional, organizational, or operational necessities, access to sensitive information or intelligence is necessary for the conduct of an individual's official duties as part of an organization that has a right to know the information in the performance of a law enforcement, homeland security, or counter-terrorism activity, such as to further an investigation or meet another law enforcement requirement.

Need to Know
(Criminal Intelligence)

Alternative definition: the determination by an authorized holder of classified information that a prospective recipient requires access to specific classified information in order to perform or assist in a lawful and authorized governmental function.

Neo-Nazi

One who desires a revival of the Nazi movement. Neo-Nazi groups are defined by their hatred for Jews and an admiration of Adolf Hitler and Nazi Germany. Although neo-Nazis also hate other minorities, homosexuals and sometimes Christians, the Jew is seen as the main enemy. Some neo-Nazis are simply racist groups, while others focus on the creation of a fascist state based on that of Nazi Germany.

Network

a structure of interconnecting components designed to communicate with each other and perform a function or functions as a unit in a specified manner.

Network
(Criminal Intelligence)

a structure of interconnecting components designed to communicate with each other and perform a function or functions as a unit in a specified manner.

Nonrepudiation
(Criminal Intelligence)

a technique used to ensure that someone performing an action on a computer cannot falsely deny that he or she performed that action. Nonrepudiation provides undeniable proof that a user took a specific action, such as transferring money, authorizing a purchase, or sending a message.

non sequitur

it does not follow; an inference that does not follow from the premises; a statement that does not follow logically from anything said.

Nuclear Material

(also called radioactive material) included all types of non-weapons-usable radioactive materials, such as cesium-137, cobalt-60, and depleted uranium, as well as weapons-usable highly enriched uranium and plutonium.

O

Odinism

Racist adherents of nature-based belief systems and long for a return to the genetically based tribe or folk. They mythologize the misty past of white northern Europeans as a romantic tableau of boar-slaying warriors, dewy-eyed Aryan maidens and pristine Alpine scenery.

Ombudsman

a government official appointed to investigate complaints made by individuals against abuses and capricious acts of public officials.

Open Communications (OPCOM)

the collection of open or publicly available communications, broadcasts, audio or video recordings, propaganda published statements and other distributed written or recorded material for purposes of analyzing the information.

Open Source Information (or Intelligence)

individual data, records, reports, and assessments that may shed light on an investigatory target or event that does not require any legal process or any type of clandestine collection techniques for a law enforcement agency to obtain. Rather, it is obtained through means that meet copyright and commercial requirements of vendors, as well as being free of legal restrictions to access by anyone who seeks that information.

Operational Analysis
(Criminal Intelligence)

an assessment of the methodology of a criminal enterprise or terrorist organization that depicts how the enterprise performs it activities, including communications, philosophy, compensation, security, and other variables that are essential for the enterprise to exist.

Operational Intelligence
(Criminal Intelligence)

information is evaluated and systematically organized on an active or potential target, such as a group of/or individual criminals, relevant premises, contact points, and methods of communication. This process is developmental in nature wherein there are sufficient articulated reasons to suspect criminal activity. Intelligence activities explore the basis of those reasons and newly developed information in order to develop a case for arrest or indictment.

Operations Security

the co-mingling of computer, technical counterintelligence security measures developed and implemented to augment traditional security programs (physical security information or personnel security and communication security) as a means of eliminating or minimizing vulnerabilities that impact on technical programs.

ORCON

A control put on intelligence products meaning "Originator Controlled." In other words, no one can use or repeat the information without the permission of the originating intelligence agency.

Originating agency
(Criminal Intelligence)

the agency or organizational entity that documents information of data, including source agencies that document SAR (and when authorized, ISE-SAR) information that is collected by a fusion center.

Outcome Evaluation
(Criminal Intelligence)

the process of determining the value or amount of success in achieving a predetermined objective through defining the objective in some qualitative or quantitative measurable terms, identifying the proper criteria (or variables) to be used in measuring the success toward attaining the objective, determination and explanation

of the degree of success, and recommendations for
further program actions to attain the desired
objectives/outcomes.

P

Paper Terrorism

involves the use of fraudulent legal documents and filings, as well as the misuse of legitimate documents and filings, in order to intimidate, harass and coerce public officials, law enforcement officers and private citizens.

People's War

Maoist term for insurgency that involves garnering popular support and employing guerrilla tactics to defeat a numerically superior force. Many terrorist groups claim to wage People's War in an effort to bring about a revolution; examples include the Communist Party of Nepal-Maoist, Shining Path in Peru, and the New People's Army of the Philippines.

per annum

in or for each year.

per capita

per unit of population; by or for each person.

per diem

a daily allowance.

per se

by, of, or in itself or oneself or themselves; as such.

**Permission
(Criminal Intelligence)**

authorization to perform operations associated with a specific shared resource, such as a file, directory, or printer. Permission must be granted by the system administrator to individual user accounts or administrative groups.

**Personal information
(Criminal Intelligence)**

information that can be used, either alone or in combination with other information, to identify individual subjects suspected of engaging in criminal activity, including terrorism.

**Personal identifiable information
(Criminal Intelligence)**

one or more pieces of information that, when considered together or in the context of how the information is presented or gathered, are sufficient to specify a unique individual. The pieces of information can be:

- Personal characteristics (such as height weight, gender, sexual orientation, date of birth, age, hair color, eye color, race, ethnicity, scars, tattoos, gang affiliation,

- religious affiliation, place of birth, mother's maiden name, distinguishing features, and retinal scans,

- A unique set of numbers or characteristics assigned to a specific individual (including name, address, phone number, social security number, e-mail address, driver's license number, financial account or credit card number and

- PIN number, Integrated Automated Fingerprint Identification System (IAFIS)

- identifier, or booking or detention system number

- Descriptions of event(s) or points in time (for example, information in documents such as police reports, arrest reports, and medical records)

- Descriptions of location(s) or place(s) (including geographic information Systems [GIS] locations, electronic bracelet monitoring information, etc.)

**Personal Identifying Information
(Criminal Intelligence)**

any information data from which a reasonable person may identify a specific individual. When Personal Identifying Information is collected, civil rights protections and privacy standards must be afforded to the document or report that contains the information.

Persons
(Criminal Intelligence)

Executive Order 12333 defines "United States persons" as United States citizens, aliens known by the intelligence agency concerned to be permanent resident aliens, an unincorporated association substantially composed of the United States citizens or permanent resident aliens, or a corporation incorporated in the United States, except for a corporation directed and controlled by a foreign government or governments. For the Intelligence Community and for domestic law enforcement agencies, "persons" means United States citizens and lawful permanent residents.

PFIAB

the President's Foreign Intelligence Advisory Board, which is a body consisting of senior non-government members appointed by, and reporting directly to the President. PFIAB is empowered to assess the quality, quantity, and adequacy of intelligence collection, of analysis and estimates, or counterintelligence, and other intelligence activities with a view toward increasing effectiveness of national intelligence effort; specific duties and responsibilities are outlined in Executive Order 12331.

Planning
(Criminal Intelligence)

the preparation for future situations, estimating organizational demands and resources needed to attend to those situations, and initiating strategies to respond to those situations.

Pointer System or Index
(Criminal Intelligence)

a system that stores information designed to identify individuals, organizations, and/or crime methodologies with the purpose of linking law enforcement agencies that have similar investigative and/or intelligence interests in the entity defined by the system.

Policy
(Criminal Intelligence)

the principles and values that guide the performance of a duty. A policy is not a statement of what must be done in a particular situation. Rather, it is a statement of guiding principles that should be followed in activities that are directed toward the attainment of goals.

Prediction
(Criminal Intelligence)

the projection of future criminal actions or changes in the nature of crime trends or a criminal enterprise based on an analysis of information depicting historical trends from which a forecast is made.

President's Daily Brief (PDB)

the President's daily published intelligence briefing delivered to him every morning.

Preventive Intelligence
(Criminal Intelligence)

intelligence that can be used to interdict or forestall a crime or terrorist attack.

Privacy
(Criminal Intelligence)

refers to individuals' interests in preventing the inappropriate collection, use, and release of personal information. Privacy interests include privacy of personal behavior, privacy of personal communications, and privacy of personal data. Other definitions of privacy include the capacity to be physically left alone (solitude); to be free from physical interference, threat, or unwanted touching (assault, battery); or to avoid being seen or overheard in particular contexts.

Privacy (Information)

the assurance that legal and constitutional restrictions on collection, maintenance, use, and disclosure of behaviors of an individual, including his/her communications, associations, and transactions, will be adhered to by criminal justice agencies, with use of such information to be strictly limited to circumstances where legal process permits use of the personally identifiable information.

Privacy (Personal)
(Criminal Intelligence)

legislation that allows an individual to review almost all federal files (and state files) under the auspices of the respective state privacy acts pertaining to him/herself, places restrictions on the disclosure of personally identifiable information, specifies that there will be no secret records systems on individuals, and compels the government to reveal its information sources.

Privacy (Personal) (Criminal Intelligence alternative definition)

the assurance that legal and constitutional restrictions on the collection, maintenance, use, and disclosure of behavior of an individual including his or her communications, associations, and transactions will be adhered to by criminal justice agencies, with use of such information strictly limited to circumstances in which legal process authorize surveillance and investigation.

Privacy Act

legislation that allows an individual to review almost all federal files pertaining to him/her, places restrictions on the disclosure of personally identifiable information, specifies that there be no secret records systems on individuals, and compels the government to reveal its information sources.

Privacy Field
(Criminal Intelligence)

a data element that may be used to identify an individual and, therefore, may be subject to privacy protection. (ISE-SAR Functional Standard.)

Privacy policy
(Criminal Intelligence)

a printed, published statement that articulates the policy position of an organization on how it handles the personal information that it gathers and uses in the normal course of business. The policy should include relating to the processes of information collection, analysis, maintenance, dissemination, and access. The purpose of the privacy policy is to articulate that the center, organization, or agency will adhere to those legal requirements and center policy determinations that enable gathering and sharing of information to occur in a manner that protects personal privacy interests. A well-developed and implemented privacy policy uses justice entity resources wisely and effectively; protects the center, organization, or agency, the individual, and the public; and promotes trust.

Privacy protection
(Criminal Intelligence)

a process of maximizing the protection of privacy, civil rights, and civil liberties when collecting and sharing information in the process of protecting public safety and public health.

Proactive
(Criminal Intelligence)

taking action that is anticipatory to a problem or situation with the intent to eliminate or mitigate the effect of the incident.

Probability

a measure of the likelihood, chance, or odds that a particular outcome or consequence will occur. This is usually expressed as a mean value between 0 and 1, with an associated minimum and maximum (range), but probability can also be expressed in qualitative terms (e.g. low, moderate, high) given that there is a common understanding of the relative meaning of the qualitative terms among all the stakeholders. The probability must be associated with a specific outcome and either a defined time frame (e.g., range of probability that a threat occurs in one year) or set of trials (e.g., range of probability of detecting a particular type of intrusion given 10 attempts).

Procedural Due Process
(Criminal Intelligence)

mandates and guarantees of law that ensure that the procedures employed to deprive a person of life, liberty, or property, during the course of the criminal justice process, meet constitutional standards.

Procedure
(Criminal Intelligence)

a method of performing an operation or a manner of proceeding on a course of action. It differs from policy in that it directs action in a particular situation to perform a specific task within the guidelines of policy. Both policies and procedures are goal-oriented. However, policies establish limits to action, whereas procedures direct response within those limits.

Profile/Criminal Profile
(Criminal Intelligence)

an investigative technique by which to identify and define the major personality and behavioral characteristics of the criminal offender based upon an analysis of the crime(s) he or she has committed.

Protected information
(Criminal Intelligence)

for the non-intelligence community, protected information is information about United States citizens and lawful permanent residents that is subject to information privacy or other legal protections under the Constitution and laws of the United States, while not within the definition established by ISE Privacy Guidelines, protection may be extended to other individuals and organizations by internal federal agency policy or regulation.

Protected information (for the federal Intelligence Community)
(Criminal Intelligence)

includes information about "United States persons" as defined in Executive Order 12333. Protected information may also include other information that the U.S. government expressly determines by Executive Order, international agreement, or other similar instrument should be covered.

Protected information (for state, local, and tribal information)
(Criminal Intelligence)

may include information about individuals and organizations that is subject to information privacy or other legal protections by law, including the U.S. Constitution; applicable federal statutes and regulations, such as civil rights laws and 28 CFTR Part 23; applicable state and tribal constitutions; and applicable state, local, and tribal laws, ordinances, and codes. Protection may be extended to other individuals and organizations by fusion center or other state, local, or tribal agency policy or regulation.

prima facie

(adv.) at first view; on first appearance. (adj) true, valid, or sufficient at first impression.

pro forma

made or carried out in a perfunctory manner or a formality.

pro rata

to divide, or distribute, or access proportionately.

Protocol (of Intelligence Collection) (Criminal Intelligence)

information collection procedures employed to obtain verbal and written information, actions of people, and physical evidence required for strategic and tactical intelligence analysis.

Public (Criminal Intelligence)

Public includes:

- Any person and any for-profit or non-profit entity, organization, or association.

- Any governmental entity for which there is no existing specific law authorizing access to the center's information.

- Media organizations.

- Entities that seek, receive, or disseminate information for whatever reason, regardless of whether it is done with the intent of making a profit, and without distinction as to the nature of intent of those requesting information from the center or participating agency.

Public does not include:

- Employees of the center or participating agency.

- People or entities, private or governmental, who assist the center in the operation of the justice information system.

- People or entities, private or governmental, who assist the center in the operation of the justice information system.

**Public Access
(Criminal Intelligence)**

relates to what information can be seen by the public; that is, information whose availability is not subject to privacy interests or rights.

**Public Value (of Information)
(Criminal Intelligence)**

intelligence or information can be released to the public when there is a need to know and a right to know the information because of the value that may be derived from public dissemination, to 1. Aid in locating targets/suspects and 2. For public safety purposes (i.e., hardening targets, taking precautions).

**Purging (Records)
(Criminal Intelligence)**

the removal and/or destruction of records because they are deemed to be of no further value or further access to the records would serve no legitimate government interests.

Q

Qualitative (Methods)

research methods that collect and analyze information which are described in narrative or rhetorical form, with conclusions drawn based on the cumulative interpreted meaning of that information.

Quantitative (Methods)

research methods that collect and analyze information that can be counted or placed on a scale of measurement that can be statistically analyzed.

quid pro quo

something for something; something given or received for something else.

R

RICO (Racketeer Influenced and Corrupt Organizations Act) (or similar state statutes) (Criminal Intelligence)

Title IX of the Organized Crime Control Act of 1970 (18 U.S.C. Sections 1961-1968) provides civil and criminal penalties for persons who engage in a pattern of racketeering activity or collection of an unlawful debt that has a specified relationship to an enterprise that affects interstate commerce.

Racketeering Activity (Criminal Intelligence)

state felonies involving murder, robbery, extortion, and several other serious offenses and more than 30 serious federal offenses, including extortion, interstate theft offenses, narcotics violations, mail fraud, and securities fraud.

Radioactive Material

(not radiological material, which does not exist) any material that undergoes nuclear decay and releases radiation. Many isotopes, such as cesium-137 and colbalt-60, are highly radioactive. However, most radioactive materials are not fissile and therefore are not weapons-usable.

Radiological Dispersal Device (RDD)

consists of a highly radioactive substance, such as cesium-137 or cobalt-60, mated to a delivery or dissemination system, such as a rocket, a bomb, or a sprayer. Uranium is not suitable for use in an RDD, which is also known as a dirty bomb.

raison d'etre

reason or justification for existence.

Raw Intelligence

a colloquial term meaning collected intelligence information that has not been converted into finished intelligence.

Reasonable Suspicion

when information exists which establishes sufficient facts to give a trained law enforcement or criminal investigative agency officer, investigator, or employee a basis to believe that there is a reasonable possibility that an individual or organization is involved in a definable criminal activity or enterprise.

Record
(Criminal Intelligence)

any item, collection, or group of information that includes personally identifiable information and is maintained, collected, used, or disseminated by or for the collecting agency or organization.

Red Mercury

fake material erroneously associated with nuclear weapons and often sold by scam artists and nuclear material traffickers.

Red Team

a technique for assessing vulnerability that involves viewing a potential target from the perspective of an attacker to identify its hidden vulnerabilities, and to anticipate possible modes of attack.

Redemption

is an ideology based on the theories of Roger Elvick, a sovereign citizen and white supremacist convicted on fraud charges in the 1980s. Redemptionists argue that by using a complicated process known as "regaining one's straw man" they can establish special Treasury Department accounts and issue bogus instruments they call "sight drafts" to pay off debts or make purchases. Should law enforcement officials interfere with this activity, redemptionists are told to file falsified I.R.S. Form 8300s against them, alleging that such officials engaged in a suspicious currency transaction. Sovereign citizen organizations like The Aware Group, Rightway L.A.W. and the Republic of Texas, among others, regularly hold Redemption seminars to teach the tactic.

Redress
(Criminal Intelligence)

laws, policies, and procedures that address public agency responsibilities with regard to access/disclosure and correction of information and the handling of complaints from persons regarding protected information about them which is under the center's, agency's, or organization's control and which is exempt from disclosure and not disclosed to the individual to whom the information pertains.

RISS (Regional Information Sharing System (Registered Trademark) (Criminal Intelligence)

RISS is composed of six regional intelligence centers that provide secure communications, information sharing resources, and investigative support to combat multijurisdictional crime and terrorist threats to more than 8,000 federal, state, local, and tribal member law enforcement agencies in all 50 states, the District of Columbia, U.S. territories, Australia, Canada, and England.

Regional Intelligence Centers (Criminal Intelligence)

multijurisdictional centers cooperatively developed within a logical geographical area that coordinate federal, state, and local law enforcement information with other information sources to track and assess criminal and terrorist threats that operating in or interacting with the region.

Reliability
(Criminal Intelligence)

asks the question, "is the source of the information consistent and dependable?"

Rendezvous

a place appointed for assembling or meeting.

Reporting
(Criminal Intelligence)

depending upon the type of intelligence, the process of placing analyzed information into the proper form to ensure the most effective consumption.

Repertoire

a list or supply of dramas, operas, pieces or parts that a company or person is prepared to perform.

Repudiation
(Criminal Intelligence)

the ability of a user to deny having performed an action that other parties cannot prove otherwise. For example, a user who deleted a file can successfully deny he deleted if no mechanism (such as audit files) can contradict that claim.

Requirements (Information or Intelligence)
(Criminal Intelligence)

the types of intelligence operation law enforcement elements need from the intelligence function within an agency (or other intelligence-producing organizations) in order for law enforcement officers to maximize protection and prevention efforts as well as identify and arrest persons who are criminally liable.

Responsibility
(Criminal Intelligence)

responsibility reflects how the authority of a unit or individual is used and determines whether goals have been accomplished and the mission fulfilled in a manner that is consistent with the defined limits of authority.

Right to Know
(Criminal Intelligence)

based on having legal authority, one's official position, legal mandates, or official agreements, allowing the individual to receive intelligence reports.

Right to privacy
(Criminal Intelligence)

the right to be left alone, in the absence of some reasonable public interest in gathering, retaining, and sharing information about a person's activities. Invasion of the right to privacy can be the basis for a lawsuit for damages against the person or entity violating a person's privacy.

Rightwing Conservative

Rightwing conservative terrorists seek to preserve the established order, or to return to the traditions of the past.

Rightwing Reactionary

terrorists who are rightwing groups that seek the overthrow of the current political order, or to return to the traditions of the past. The Klu Klux Klan, for example, wants the American south to return to its pre-Civil War social order.

Risk Management Based Intelligence (Criminal Intelligence)

an approach to intelligence analysis that has as its objective the calculation of risk attributable to a threat source or acts threatened by a threat source; a means of providing strategic intelligence for planning and policy making especially regarding vulnerabilities and countermeasures designed to prevent criminal acts; a means of providing tactical or operational intelligence in support of operations against a specific threat source, capacity or modality; can be quantitative if a proper data base exists to measure likelihood, impact and calculate risk; can be qualitative, subjective and still deliver a reasonable reliable ranking of risk for resource allocation and other decision making in strategic planning and or operations in tactical situations.

Risk Assessment

The process of analyzing threats to and vulnerability of a facility, determining the potential for losses and identifying cost effective corrective measures and residual risk.

Risk Assessment
(Criminal Intelligence)

risk is defined as the product of three principal variables:

1. **Threat** (the likelihood of an attack occurring)

2. **Vulnerability**

3. **Consequences** (the relative exposure and expected impact of an attack).

Risk assessment is the process of expected impact of an attack. Risk assessment is the process of qualitatively or quantitatively determining the probability of an adverse event and the severity of its impact on an asset. It is a function of threat, vulnerability, and consequence. A risk assessment may include scenarios in which two more risks interact to create or lessen impact. A risk assessment provides the basis for the rank ordering of risks and for establishing priorities for countermeasures.

Risk is classically represented as the product of a probability of a particular outcome and the results of that outcome. A statewide or regional assessment of the threats, vulnerabilities, and consequences faced by a fusion center's geographic area responsibility. The risk is used to identify priority information requirements for the fusion center and to support urban area homeland security preparedness planning efforts to allocate funding, capabilities, and other resources.

In traditional criminal intelligence, a risk assessment means an analysis of a target, illegal commodity, or victim to identify the probability of being attacked or criminally compromised and to analyze vulnerabilities.

Risk Management-Based Intelligence (Criminal Intelligence)

Risk management is a continual process or cycle in which risks are identified, measured, and evaluated; countermeasures are then designed, implemented, and monitored to see how they perform, with continual feedback loops for decision-maker input to improve countermeasures and consider tradeoffs between risk acceptance and avoidance.

Risk Management-Based Intelligence (Criminal Intelligence)

risk management is also defined as an approach to intelligence analysis that has as it object the calculation of the risk attributable to a threat source or acts threatened by a threat source. It also is a means of providing strategic intelligence for planning and policymaking, especially regarding vulnerabilities and countermeasures designed to prevent criminal acts. And it is a means of providing tactical or operational intelligence in support of operations against a specific threat source, capability, or modality; can be quantitative if a proper database exists to measure likelihood and impact and calculate risk. Risk Management-Based Intelligence can be qualitative and subjective and still deliver a reasonably reliable ranking of risk for resource allocation and other decision making in strategic planning and for operations in tactical situations.

Role-based access
(Criminal Intelligence)

a type of access authorization that uses roles to determine access rights and privileges. A role is a symbolic category of users that share the same security privilege.

Rule
(Criminal Intelligence)

a specific requirement or prohibition that is stated to prevent deviations from policy or procedure. A violation of a rule typically results in an internal investigation and my result in disciplinary action.

SCI (Sensitive Compartmented Information)

S

SCI (Sensitive Compartmented Information)

classified information concerning or derived from intelligence sources, methods, or analytical processes that is required to be handled within formal access control systems.

SCIF (Sensitive Compartmented Information Facility)

an accredited area, room, group of rooms, buildings, or an installation where SCI may be stored, used, discussed, and/or processed.

Safe-haven

The term is used by the Intelligence Community to describe a range of situations involving a terrorist presence in a country. Some situations include those where there is no government; where government actions are weak or ineffective; where the government turns a blind eye; where governments actively protect and collaborate with terrorists such as Afghanistan under the Taliban; and where the government is run by terrorists. A safe-haven involves well-established

184

terrorist network infrastructure; staging areas; hubs used for terrorist activity.

Sealing (Records)
(Criminal Intelligence)

records stored by an agency that cannot be accessed, referenced, or used without a court order or statutory authority based on a showing of evidence that there is a legitimate government interest to review the sealed information.

SAR (Suspicious Activity Report) (Financial Intelligence)

a report of suspicious activity regarding money orders, traveler's checks, and money transfer transactions. The Suspicious Activity Report was created by the Money Services Business (MSB) and has been designed specifically for use by MSBs.

SAR (Suspicious Activity Report)
(Criminal Intelligence)

official documentation of reported or observed activity and/or behavior that, based on an officer's training and experience, is believed to be indicative of intelligence gathering or preoperational planning related to terrorism, criminal, or other illicit intention. (*Findings and Recommendations of the Suspicious Activity Report (SAR) Support and Implementation Report*, June 2008; and ISE SAR Functional Standard version 1.0)

Secret Classification

applied to information, the unauthorized disclosure of which reasonably could be expected to cause serious damage to the national security that the original classification authority is able to identify or describe.

Sectarianism

a narrow-minded adherence to a particular sect (political, ethnic, or religious), often leading to conflict with those of different sects or possessing different beliefs. Sectarian conflicts are often breeding grounds for acts of terrorism and the formation of terrorist groups.

Sector Coordinating Councils (SCCs) (Criminal Intelligence)

serve as the government's principal point of entry into each sector for the purpose of addressing the entire range of CIKR protection and risk management issues. While they are supported and facilitated by DHS and the sector-specific agency, SCCs are self-organized entities composed of a broad base sector infrastructure owner-operators and their representatives from sector trade associations. Often chaired by a sector owner-operator SCCs serve as "honest brokers" to facilitate sector-wide organization and coordination of a sector's CIKR protection policy development, planning, and program implementation and monitoring activities. Each SCC identifies, coordinates and supports the information sharing principles, needs, and capabilities most appropriate for its sector as required by HSPD-7.

Security
(Criminal Intelligence)

refers to the range of administrative, technical, and physical business practices and mechanisms that aim to preserve privacy and confidentiality by restricting information access to authorized users for authorized purposes. Computer and communications security efforts also have the goal of ensuring the accuracy and timely availability of data for the legitimate user set, as well as promoting failure resistance in the electronic systems overall.

Security (Criminal Justice Commission, 1995)

a series of procedures and measures that, when combined provide protection of people from harm, information from improper disclosure or alteration, and assets from theft damage.

SBU (Sensitive But Unclassified Information) (Criminal Intelligence)

refers collectively to the various designations used, prior to the issuance of the Controlled Unclassified Information network, within the federal government for documents and information that are sufficiently sensitive to warrant some level of protection from disclosure but that do not warrant classification. (Presidential Memorandum to Heads of Executive Departments and Agencies, Designation and Sharing of Controlled Unclassified Information (CUI), May 7, 2008.)

Sensitive Compartmented Information Facility (Criminal Intelligence)

an accredited area, room, group of rooms, buildings, or an installation where SCI may be stored, used discussed, and/or processed.

SBU (Sensitive But Unclassified Information)

information that has not been classified by a federal law enforcement agency which pertains to significant law enforcement cases under investigation and criminal intelligence reports that require dissemination criteria to only those persons necessary to further the investigation or to prevent a crime or terrorist act.

SHSI (Sensitive Homeland Security Information) (Criminal Intelligence)

information created or received by an agency or any local, county, state, or tribal government that the loss misuse, unauthorized disclosure, modification of, or the unauthorized access to could reasonably be expected to significantly impair the capabilities and/or efforts of agencies and/or local, county, state, and tribal personnel to predict analyze, investigate, deter, prevent, protect, against, mitigate the effects of, or recover from acts of terrorism. SHSI does not include information that is: Classified as a national security, information pursuant to Executive Order12958, as amended or any successor order. Designated by Executive Order 12951, any successor order, or the Atomic Energy Act of 1954 (42 U.S.C. 2011), to acquire protection against unauthorized disclosure. Protected Critical Infrastructure

Information (PCII) as defined in 6 CFR Part 29.2.4.Sensitive Security Information (SSI) as defined in 49 CFR Part 1520.

SCI (Sensitive Compartmented Information)

classified information concerning or derived from intelligence sources, methods, or analytical processes that is required to be handled within formal access control systems established by the director of the Central Intelligence Agency.

SCI (Sensitive Compartmented Information) (Criminal Intelligence)

classified information concerning or derived from intelligence sources, methods, or analytical processes that is required to be handled within formal access control systems.

SHSI (Sensitive Homeland Security Information)

any information created or received by an agency or any local, county, state, or tribal government that the loss, misuse, unauthorized disclosure, modification of, or the unauthorized access to, could reasonably be expected to impair significantly the capabilities and/or efforts of agencies and/or local, county, state, and tribal personnel to predict, analyze, investigate, deter, prevent, protect against, mitigate the effects of or recover from acts of terrorism. SHSI does not include any information that is:

1. Classified as national security information pursuant to Executive Order 12958, as amended, or any successor order.

2. Designed by Executive Order 12951, any successive order, or the Atomic Energy Act of 1954, to require protection against unauthorized disclosure.

3. Protected Critical Infrastructure Information (PCII) as defined in 6 Code of Federal Regulation (CFR) 29.2.

4. Sensitive Security Information (SSI) as defined in 49 CFR Part 1520.

Sharia

a system of Islamic law derived from the Quran and the practices of the Prophet Mohammed. Islamist terrorist group groups often see the establishment of Sharia as an end-goal, although actual Sharia law is generally seen as antithetical to terrorist practices.

SIGINT (Signals Intelligence)

the interception of various radio frequency signals, microwave signals, satellite audio communications, non-imagery infrared and coherent light signals, and transmissions from surreptitiously placed audio micro-transmitters in support of the communications intelligence activity.

SIGINT (Signals intelligence)

Alternative definition: intelligence information derived from signals intercept comprising, either individually or in combination with, all communications intelligence, electronic intelligence, and foreign instrument signals intelligence however transmitted.

sin qua non

an absolutely indispensable or essential thing.

Sleeper Cell

a unit of terrorists that integrates into a city or region but lies dormant until it receives orders to carry out an attack.

Social Totalitarianism

a modern fascist philosophy, which differs significantly from fascism of World War II. Some neo-fascists shifted away from the traditional highly centralized approach to political power and toward plans to fragment and subdivide political authority. Industrial-era totalitarianism relied on the nation-state; in the era of outsourcing, deregulation, and global mobility, social totalitarianism looked to local authorities, private bodies (such as churches), and direct mass activism to enforce repressive control.

Source agency
(Criminal Intelligence)

refers to the agency organizational entity that originates SAR (and when authorized, ISE-SAR) information.

Sources

The word source usually refers to a human (clandestine) source and is often accompanied by words such as reliable, untested, etc. to give the reader an idea of reliability. At times, just the word HUMINT is used, meaning a person. Theses sources collect or possess critical information needed for intelligence analysis.

Sources
(Criminal Intelligence)

from an intelligence perspective, these are persons (human intelligence or HUMINT) who collect or process critical information needed for intelligence analysis.

Soft Target

a target that is relatively unguarded or difficult to protect from terrorists, and therefore yields a higher probability for a successful attack. Examples include: subways, storage facilities, pharmaceutical companies, entertainment venues, parks, and schools.

Sovereign Citizen Movement

a loosely organized collection of groups and individuals who have adopted a right-wing anarchist ideology originating in the theories of a group called Posse Comitatus in the 1970s. Its adherents believe that virtually all existing government in the United States is illegitimate and they seek to "restore" an idealized, minimalist government and other forms of authority using "paper terrorism" harassment and intimidation tactics, and occasionally resorting to violence.

Spatial Analysis

the process of using a geographic information system in combination with crime analysis techniques to assess the geographic context of offenders, crimes, and other law enforcement activity or intelligence analysis.

SSCI (Senate Select Committee on Intelligence)

a select committee of the Senate established by Senate Resolution 400, 94th Congress, 2nd Session (1976), whose function is to monitor and provide oversight of the Intelligence Community and intelligence related activities of all other government organizations; the Committee is also responsible for legislation pertaining to intelligence agencies and activities, including authorizing appropriations for such activities.

Suspicious activity
(Criminal Intelligence)

defined in the ISE-SAR Functional Standard (Version 1.5) as "observed behavior reasonably indicative of preoperational planning related to terrorism or other criminal activity." Examples of suspicious activity include surveillance, photography of sensitive infrastructure facilities, site breach or physical intrusion, cyber attacks, and testing of security.

Suspicious Activity Report (SAR) (Criminal Intelligence)

Official documentation of observed behavior reasonably indicative of preoperational planning related to terrorism or other criminal activity. Suspicious activity report (SAR) information offers a standardized means for feeding information repositories or data analysis tools. Patterns identified during SAR information analysis may be investigated in coordination with the reporting agency and, if applicable, a state or regional fusion center. SAR information is not intended to be used to track or record ongoing enforcement, intelligence, or investigatory activities, nor is it designed to support interagency calls for service.

State-sponsored Terrorism

countries determined by the Secretary of State to have repeatedly provided support for acts of international terrorism are designed pursuant to three laws: section 6(j) of the Export Administration Act, section 40 of the Arms Export Control Act, and section 620A of the Foreign Assistance Act. Taken together, the four main categories of sanctions resulting from designation under these authorities include restrictions on U.S. foreign assistance; a ban on defense exports and sales; certain controls over exports of dual use items; and miscellaneous financial and other restrictions." (U.S. State Department Definition)

Statistical System

an organized means of collecting, processing, storing, and retrieving aggregate information for the purposes of analysis, research, or reference.

Strategic Intelligence

an assessment of targeted crime patterns, crime trends, criminal organizations, and/or unlawful commodity transactions for purposes of planning, decision making, and resource allocation; the focused examination of unique, pervasive, and/or complex crime or intelligence problems.

Substantive Due Process (Criminal Intelligence)

guarantees persons against arbitrary governmental actions so that no government agency may exercise powers beyond those authorized by the Constitution.

Suicide Bombing

any attempt to detonate an explosive device to harm people or damage property in which the assailant neither wishes nor expects to survive. The bomber's purpose is to be able to retain ultimate control over the timing and location of detonation.

Surveillance
(Criminal Intelligence)

the observation of activities, behaviors, and associations of LAWINT target (individual or group) with the intent to gather incriminating information, or "lead" information, which is used for the furtherance of a criminal investigation.

Suspicious activity
(Criminal Intelligence)

reported or observed activity and/or behavior that, based on an officer's training and experience, is believed to be indicative of intelligence gathering or preoperational planning related terrorism, criminal, or other illicit intention. *(Findings and Recommendations of the Suspicious Activity Report (SAR) Support and implementation Project 2008; and ISE-SAR Functional Standard version 1.0)*

Suspicious Activity Report
(Criminal Intelligence)

a report and process wherein criminal indicators and behaviors that appear to have a criminal nexus are documented and processed through a law enforcement organization to determine if a crime is being planned, in the process of being committed or has been committed.

T

Tactical Intelligence

evaluated information on which immediate enforcement action can be based; furtherance of a criminal investigation or battlefield plan. Intelligence produced in support of military, intelligence, or other operations, or that relates to the specific time, date, nature, and other details of an event.

Takfir

the practice of declaring that an individual or group previously considered Muslim are non-believers in Allah; usually applies to the judgment that an action has been taken by a Muslim that indicates abandonment of Islam or Islamic beliefs. The sentence for apostasy (takfir) under traditionally interpreted Sharia is execution.

Target

an asset, or one or more systems, subsystems or other endeavor within an asset that a threat is intended to disrupt damage, or destroy.

Target
(Criminal Intelligence)

any person, organization, group, crime or criminal series or commodity being subject to investigation analysis.

Target Capabilities List (TCL)
(Criminal Intelligence)

a component of the *National Preparedness Guidelines,* which describe the collective national capabilities required to prevent, protect against, respond to, and recover from terrorist attacks, major disasters, and other emergencies. The Guidelines use a capabilities-based preparedness approach to planning. Simply put, a capability provides the means to accomplish a mission. Some capabilities cut across all mission areas and are therefore placed in a Common Mission Area. Relevant Target Capabilities for fusion centers include:

- Intelligence/Information Sharing and Dissemination (Common Area Mission)

- Risk Management (Common)

- Information Gathering and Recognition of Indicators and Warning (Prevent)

- Intelligence Analysis and Production (Prevent)

- Counter-Terror Investigation and Law Enforcement (Prevent)

- Law Enforcement Investigation and Operations (Prevent)

In addition some fusion centers' defined missions support and other capabilities, such as:

- Critical Infrastructure Protection (Prevent)

- Epidemiological Surveillance and Investigation (Protect)

- Food and Agriculture Safety and Defense (Protect)

- Public Safety and Security Response (Response)

- CBNE Detection (Prevent)

Note: The *Target Capabilities List* should be viewed as a reference document or guide to preparedness. The TCL is available for review at www.llis.dhs.gov.

Target Profile
(Criminal Intelligence)

a profile that is person-specific and contains sufficient detail to initiate a target operation or support an ongoing operation against an individual or networked group of individuals.

Targeting
(Criminal Intelligence)

the identification of crimes, crime trends, and crime patterns that have discernable characteristics which make collection and analysis of intelligence information an efficient and effective method for identifying, apprehending, and prosecuting those who are criminally responsible.

Tawhid

is an Islamic term in Arabic meaning "monotheism."
Monotheism is an important part of the Islamic faith
(as well as other major religions), and Islamist terrorists
often co-opt the term for group names in an effort to
show piety.

Tear Line

the place on an intelligence report (usually denoted by a
series of dashes) at which the sanitized, less-classified
version of a more highly classified and/or controlled
report begins. The sanitized information below the tear
line should contain the substance of the information
above the tear line but without identifying the sensitive
sources and methods. This will permit wider
dissemination, in accordance with the "need-to-know"
principle and foreign disclosure guidelines, of the
information below the tear line. Typically the
information below the tear line can be released as
sensitive but unclassified.

**Tear-Line Report
(Criminal Intelligence)**

a report containing classified intelligence or
information that is prepared in such a manner that data
relating to intelligence sources and methods are easily
removed from the report to protect sources and
methods from disclosure. Typically, the information
below the "tear line" can be released as sensitive but
unclassified.

Telemetry
(Criminal Intelligence)

the collection and processing of information derived from non-communications electromagnetic radiations emitting from sources such as radio navigation systems (e.g., transponders), radar systems, and information/data signals emitted from monitoring equipment in a vehicle or device.

Telephone Record (Toll)/Communications
Analysis
(Criminal Intelligence)

an assessment of telephone call activity associated with investigatory targets to include telephone numbers called and/or received, the frequency of calls between numbers the dates of calls, length of calls, and patterns of use.

Terrorism

is violence, threat of violence, calculated to create an atmosphere of fear or alarm. These acts are designed to coerce others into actions they would not otherwise undertake, or refrain from actions they desired to take. All terrorist acts are crimes. Many would also be violation of the rules of war if a state of war existed.

This violence or threat of violence is generally directed against civilian targets. The motives of all terrorists are political, and terrorist actions are generally carried out in a way that will achieve maximum publicity. Unlike other criminal acts, terrorists claim credit for their acts.

Finally, terrorist acts are intended to produce effects beyond the immediate physical damage of the cause, having long-term psychological repercussions on a particular target audience. The fear created by terrorists may be intended to cause people to exaggerate the strengths of the terrorist and the importance of the cause, to provoke governmental overreaction, to discourage dissent, or simply to intimate and thereby enforce compliance with their demands.

Terrorism information
(Criminal Intelligence)

consistent with Section 1016(a)(4) of the Intelligence Reform and Terrorism Prevention Act of 2004 (IRTPA), all information relating to (a) the existence, organization, capabilities, plans, intentions, vulnerabilities, means of finance or material support, or activities of foreign or international terrorist groups or individuals or domestic groups, or individuals involved in transnational terrorism; (b) threats posed by such groups or individuals to the United States, United States persons, or United States interests or to those interests of other nations; (c) communications of or by such groups or individuals; or (d) other groups or individuals reasonably believed to be assisting or associated with such groups or individuals.

Terrorism-related information
(Criminal Intelligence)

in accordance with the Intelligence Reform and Terrorism Prevention Act of 2004 (IRTPA), as amended by the 9/11 Commission Act (August 3, 2007, P.L. 110-53), the ISE facilitates the sharing of terrorism and homeland security information, as defined in IRTPA Section 1016(a)(5) and the Homeland Security Act (892)(f)(1) (6 U.S.C. 482(f)(1). See also *Information Sharing Environment Implementation Plan* (November 2006) and Presidential Guidelines 2 and 3 (the ISE will facilitate the sharing of "terrorism information," as defined in the IRTPA, as well as the following categories of information to the extent that they do not otherwise constitute "terrorism information":

1. homeland security information as defined in Section 892(f)(1) of the Homeland Security Act of 2002 (6 U.S.C. 482(f)(1); and
2. law enforcement information relating to terrorism or the security of our homeland. Such additional information may include intelligence information.

Terrorist Group

a collection of individuals belonging to an autonomous non-state or sub-national revolutionary or anti-government movement who are dedicated to the use of violence to achieve their objectives. Such an entity is seen as having at least some structural and command and control apparatus that, no matter how loose or flexible, nonetheless provides an overall organizational framework and general strategic direction. This definition is meant to include contemporary religion-motivated and apocalyptic groups and other movements that seek theological justification or divine sanction for their acts of violence.

Terrorist

an adversary who attacks an asset to cause fear for political gain. Someone who uses unlawful force or violence against persons or property to intimidate or coerce a government or civilian population in furtherance of political or social objectives.

tete-a-tete

a private conversation between two persons.

Third-Agency Rule
(Criminal Intelligence)

an agreement wherein a source agency releases information under the condition that the receiving agency does not release the information to any other agency that is, a third agency.

Third Position

A political ideology that emphasizes the commonalities between the extreme left and the extreme right, groups that have found themselves fighting side by side against globalization in recent years. The Third Position incorporates anti-Semitic extremism of the hard right with traditionally leftist ideas and tactics. Third Positionists advocate a redistribution of wealth, a ban on animal testing, and respect for the environment. Third Positionists seek to overthrow existing governments and replace them with monocultural nation states built around the idea of supremacist racial nationalism and/or supremacist religious nationalism.

Third Position neofascists have organized in the U.S., Europe, and Middle East, and they maintain some kind of loose network, at least for the purposes of discussing their shared ideas and agenda, but in some cases involving meetings and even funding.

Threat Assessment

the process to identity threat categories and adversaries, assessing the intent of each adversary, the capability of each adversary, the frequency of past incidents and an estimation of the threat relative to each critical asset.

Threat Assessment (alternate definition)

is used to evaluate the likelihood of terrorist activity against a given asset or location. It is a decision support tool that helps to establish and prioritize security-program requirements, planning, and resource allocations. A threat assessment identifies and evaluates each threat on the basis of various factors, including capability, intention and lethality of an attack.

Threat Assessment (Criminal Intelligence)

an assessment of a criminal or terrorist presence within a jurisdiction integrated with an assessment of potential targets of that presence and a statement of probability that the criminal or terrorist will commit an unlawful act. The assessment focuses on the criminal's or terrorist's opportunity, capability, and willingness to fulfill the threat.

Threat Analysis

In antiterrorism, threat analysis is a continual process of compiling and examining all available information concerning potential terrorist activity by terrorist groups that could target a facility. A threat analysis will review the factors of a terrorist group's existence, capacity, intentions, history, and targeting, as well as the security environment within which friendly forces operate. Threat analysis is an essential step in identifying probability of terrorist attack and results in a threat assessment.

Threat

any indication, circumstance, or event with the potential to cause the loss of, or damage to, an asset. Threat can also be defined as the intention and capability of an adversary to understand actions that would be detrimental to assets.

Threat Inventory (Criminal Intelligence)

an information and intelligence-based survey within the region of a law enforcement agency to identify potential individuals or groups that pose a criminal or terrorist threat without a judgment of the kind of threat they pose. The inventory is simply to determine their presence.

THREATCON (Terrorist Threat Conditions)

The Chairman of the Joint Chiefs of Staff-approved program standardizing the military services' identification of recommended responses to terrorist threats against U.S. personnel and facilities. This program is designed to facilitate inter-service coordination and support for antiterrorist activities. There are four THREATCONS above normal:

THREATCON ALPHA applies to a condition when there is a general threat of possible terrorist activity against personnel and facilities, the nature and extent of which are unpredictable and circumstances do not justify full implementation of **THREATCON BRAVO** measures. However, it may be necessary to implement certain measures from higher THREATCONS resulting from intelligence received or as a deterrent. The measures in this THREATCON must be capable of being maintained indefinitely.

THREATCON BRAVO is a condition that applies when an increased and more predictable threat of terrorist activity exits. The measures for this THREATCON must be capable of being maintained for weeks without causing hardship, affecting operational capability, and aggravating relations with local authorities.

THREATCON CHARLIE is a condition that applies when an incident occurs or intelligence is received indicating some form of terrorist action against U.S. personnel and facilities is imminent. Implementation of measures in this THREATCON for more than a short period probably will create hardship and affect the peacetime activities of the unit and its personnel.

THREATCON DELTA is a condition that applies in the immediate area where a terrorist action against a specific location or person is likely. Normally, this THREATCON is declared as a localized condition.

Title III Order

an order issued by a court pursuant to the provisions of Title III of the Omnibus Crime Control and Safe Streets Act of 1968, Public Law 90-351 (June 19, 1968), as amended, authorizing the interception of oral, wire, and/or electronic communication.

Top Secret Classification

applied to information, the unauthorized disclosure of which reasonably could be expected to cause serious damage to the national security that the original classification authority is able to identify or describe.

tour de force

a feat of strength, skill, or ingenuity.

Turner Diaries

racist novel written by William Turner n 1978. The book was an inspiration for violent white supremacist groups such as "The New Order" as well as Timothy McVeigh. The book describes the futuristic United States consumed by an all-out race war.

U

USA PATRIOT Act

Uniting and Strengthening America by Providing Appropriate Tools Required to Intercept and Obstruct Terrorism Act of 2001

Umma (Ummah)

people of Islam; the Arabic word for "community" that is ordained to be temporally and geopolitically victorious at history's end.

Undercover Investigation (Criminal Intelligence)

active infiltration (or attempt to infiltrate) a group believed to be involved in criminal activity and/or the interaction with a LAWINT target with the intent to gather incriminating information that is used for the furtherance of criminal investigation.

Uranium Enrichment

natural uranium consists of approximately 0.7 uranium-235 and 99.3 percent uranium-238. Uranium with a lower percentage of uranium-235 is referred to as depleted uranium. **Uranium** with a uranium-235 content below 20 percent is referred to as low enriched uranium. Uranium with a uranium-235 content of more than 20 percent is referred to as highly enriched uranium. In all cases, all uranium (even depleted uranium) is slightly radioactive.

V

Validity
(Criminal Intelligence)

asks the question, "Does the information actually represent what we believe it represents?"

Variable
(Criminal Intelligence)

any characteristic on which individuals, groups, items, or incidents differ.

Vet

to vet a proposal, source, work product, or concept to an appraisal by command personnel and/or experts to ascertain accuracy, consistency, and/or feasibility before proceeding.

vice versa

with the order changed.

Violent Criminal Apprehension Program (VICAP) Criminal Intelligence)

a nationwide data information center operated by the FBI's National Center for the Analysis of Violent Crime, designed to collect, collate, and analyze specific crimes of violence.

vis-à-vis

one that is face to face with another; face to face; as compared with; in relation to.

Vulnerability

is the susceptibility of resources to negative impacts from hazard events; a weakness in defenses; capable of or susceptible to being wounded or hurt, as by a weapon: *a vulnerable part of the body*; open to moral attack, criticism, temptation, etc.: *an argument vulnerable to refutation; He is vulnerable to bribery*; (of a place) open to assault; difficult to defend: a vulnerable bridge.

Vulnerability Assessment

is a process that indicates weaknesses in physical structures, personnel protection systems, processes, or other areas that may be exploited by terrorists and may suggest options to eliminate or mitigate those weaknesses.

Vulnerability Assessment
(Criminal Intelligence)

an assessment of possible criminal or terrorist group targets within a jurisdiction integrated with an assessment of the target's weakness, likelihood of being attacked, and ability to withstand an attack.

W

Wahhabism

an Islamic "reform movement" to restore "pure monotheistic worship", or an "extremist pseudo-Sunni movement". Adherents often object to the term Wahhabi or Wahhabism as derogatory, and prefer to be called *Salafi* or *muwahhid*.

Warning
(Criminal Intelligence)

to notify in advance of possible harm or victimization as a result of information and intelligence gained concerning the probability of a crime or terrorist attack.

Weapons of Mass Destruction (WMD)
(Criminal Intelligence)

information was defined and included in the definition of "terrorism information" by P.L. 110-53. Weapons of Mass Destruction. Weapons that through their use or threat of use can cause large-scale damage and contamination, shifts in military objectives, phases or courses of action. Nuclear, radiological, biological, and chemical weapons are weapons of mass destruction.

Weapons-usable Nuclear Material

fissile material that is suitable for a nuclear device. For practical purposes, this includes only highly enriched uranium and plutonium-239. This term is specific to a nuclear device and is not used to describe materials that are usable in a radiological dispersal device.

WIRe (World Intellience Review)

a daily Intelligence Community analytical product that is circulated electronically

About the Author

David Cariens is a retired CIA officer--31-year career. Most of his time at the Agency was spent as a political analyst dealing with Eastern Europe. In this capacity he wrote for all levels of the U.S. government--from the President to the working level analysts and policymakers.

He served as an officer overseas in Eastern Europe and as an editor at the BBC/FBIS facility outside London. He headed the CIA University program to teach new analysts writing and briefing skills. He also served on the CIA's Inspector General's staff.

Cariens currently teaches Intelligence Analysis and Writing for the Intelligence Community. In addition to his work in the U.S., Cariens teaches intelligence and crime analysis for the Royal Canadian Mounted Police, the Correctional Service of Canada, and he has taught for the Singapore Police.

Cariens served as a member of the Ad-hoc Program Advisory Committee (PAC) relative to the development of the Bachelor of Applied Public Safety (BAPS) - Specialization in Crime and Intelligence Analysis at Seneca College, Toronto, Canada.

Cariens teaches a course at the University of Richmond's Osher Institute entitled, "What Should We Expect From Intelligence."

He is the author of "A Question of Accountability: The Murder of Angela Dales" -- an examination of the shooting at the Appalachian School of Law in Grundy, Virginia in January 2002. Angela Dales, the mother of Cariens' oldest grandchild, was killed in that shooting. His textbook, "Critical Thinking Through Writing: Intelligence and Crime Analysis" is currently available through Lulu.com, Amazon.com, and other retailers. They are also available on Kindle. Cariens is a contributing author to the International Association of Law Enforcement Intelligence Agency's "Criminal Intelligence for the 21st Century."

Cariens is a victim's rights advocate (all volunteer) working with the victims of the Virginia Tech tragedy. He takes no money for his work on behalf of school shooting victims and their families. He is the author of "Virginia Tech: Make Sure It Doesn't Get Out," was published in January, 2014. Cariens' new textbook, "A Handbook for Intelligence and Crime Analysts" is slated for publication in mid-2015